Let Us Go!

A Complete Beginner's Guide to Golang Programming and Development

Rahul Sid Patil

Apress®

Let Us Go!: A Complete Beginner's Guide to Golang Programming and Development

Rahul Sid Patil
Pune, Maharashtra, India

ISBN-13 (pbk): 979-8-8688-1441-9   ISBN-13 (electronic): 979-8-8688-1442-6
https://doi.org/10.1007/979-8-8688-1442-6

Copyright © 2025 by Rahul Sid Patil

Managing Director, Apress Media LLC: Welmoed Spahr
Acquisitions Editor: Anandadeep Roy
Editorial Assistant: Jessica Vakili

Cover designed by eStudioCalamar

Cover image designed by Freepik (www.freepik.com)

Distributed to the book trade worldwide by Springer Science+Business Media New York, 1 New York Plaza, New York, NY 10004. Phone 1-800-SPRINGER, fax (201) 348-4505, e-mail orders-ny @springer-sbm.com, or visit www.springeronline.com. Apress Media, LLC is a Delaware LLC and the sole member (owner) is Springer Science + Business Media Finance Inc (SSBM Finance Inc). SSBM Finance Inc is a **Delaware** corporation.

For information on translations, please e-mail booktranslations@springernature.com; for reprint, paperback, or audio rights, please e-mail bookpermissions@springernature.com.

Apress titles may be purchased in bulk for academic, corporate, or promotional use. eBook versions and licenses are also available for most titles. For more information, reference our Print and eBook Bulk Sales web page at http://www.apress.com/bulk-sales.

Any source code or other supplementary material referenced by the author in this book is available to readers on GitHub. For more detailed information, please visit https://www.apress.com/gp/services/source-code.

If disposing of this product, please recycle the paper

I dedicate this book to all the budding Gophers and cloud-native developers who are shaping the future of modern, intelligent, and cloud-native enterprise software. Your passion and innovation are building the foundation for a smarter and more connected world, driving technology to make life better for humankind. May this book serve as a guide and inspiration on your journey.

Table of Contents

About the Author

 **Rahul Sid Patil** is a seasoned software engineer and thought leader with more than a decade of experience in Golang, cloud-native development, and distributed systems. As the Head of the Golang Community at EPAM Systems, India, he plays a pivotal role in fostering collaboration and innovation within the developer ecosystem.

A dynamic public speaker, Rahul has shared his expertise at prestigious international tech events, including the Great Indian Developer Summit (GIDS). He has also served as a mentor and jury member at the Smart India Hackathon, one of the world's largest hackathons, inspiring and guiding the next generation of tech talent.

Rahul is a popular author on Medium, where he writes on software development and modern technology practices, and an open source contributor known for the "crongen" library. He is the founder of the Cloud Native Developer's Forum (CNDF), a YouTube channel dedicated to educating developers on cloud-native technologies.

About the Technical Reviewer

Pranav Manole is a seasoned web developer with experience in working with various web technologies. He's been working in the IT industry for more than 7.5 years. Currently, he is working as a Senior Software Engineer at Victoria's Secret & Co., Bangalore. For the past four years, he has been actively working in Golang and exploring various aspects of it. He feels Golang, one of the most widely accepted languages, is very easy to learn. Due to its key features like concurrency, memory management, error handling, and most importantly simplicity, it is getting popular in the IT industry. He feels this book is written in such a way that the reader will find it engaging due to the question-and-answer structure. The what, why, where, and how of Golang concepts are explained in a systematic way.

Acknowledgments

I would like to extend my heartfelt gratitude to the following people who have played a crucial role in making this book a reality:

- **Anandadeep Roy**, editor (web development and open source), for giving me the opportunity to write this book and for his invaluable guidance throughout the process

- **Deepa Shirley Tryphosa**, project coordinator for this book, for her patient follow-ups and insightful inputs that helped shape this work

- **Pranav Manole**, Senior Software Engineer at Victoria's Secret & Co., for his thorough and on-point technical review, ensuring the quality and accuracy of the content

- **My family**—my wife Bhagyashree, my daughter Urvi, and my mother Nandini—for their unwavering support and understanding of my lack of availability for the family during this project

Without their encouragement and dedication, this book would not have been possible.

Introduction

Welcome to *Let Us Go!*, your practical guide to mastering Go programming! This book is designed to help you navigate the fundamentals of Go, a modern programming language that's transforming the way developers build scalable, efficient, and high-performance applications.

Whether you are

A beginner programmer with little to no prior experience in Go but eager to learn with clear, step-by-step guidance

A student seeking a comprehensive resource to supplement your coursework and apply programming concepts through hands-on projects

A self-taught developer transitioning into professional Go development, looking for a structured approach and practical examples

A hobbyist or enthusiast keen on exploring a new language and building projects you can showcase

A professional developer aiming to upskill and leverage Go's capabilities for enterprise-level software

this book is tailored to make your learning journey engaging, interactive, and rewarding.

Why Golang Is the Future of Enterprise Software Development

In the fast-paced world of enterprise software development, efficiency, scalability, and maintainability are paramount. With modern businesses demanding robust, high-performance applications that can scale seamlessly in cloud environments, development teams are reevaluating their language choices. Enter Golang—a language that's not just a tool but a game-changer. Here's why enterprise software development companies are increasingly turning to Golang to build the future.

The Rise of Golang: An Overview

Developed by Google in 2007 and released to the public in 2009, Golang (or simply Go) was designed to address the challenges of modern software development. With a syntax reminiscent of C, combined with modern programming constructs, Golang was created to balance simplicity and power. Today, it's the language behind some of the most critical systems, including Kubernetes, Docker, and Prometheus.

Why Enterprises Love Golang

1. Blazing Performance Without Complexity

Compiled Language: Golang compiles directly to machine code, eliminating the overhead of runtime interpretation. This translates to faster execution times and better resource utilization.

Optimized for Concurrency: In Go, a **goroutine** is a lightweight way to perform multiple tasks at the same time. Imagine cooking dinner while the washing machine is running—**goroutines** allow your program to handle such multitasking effortlessly. You'll get hands-on experience with **goroutines** when we cover concurrency in later chapters.

Garbage Collection: This is an automatic process that cleans up unused memory while your program is running. Think of it as a janitor that ensures your application runs smoothly without you having to manually manage memory. Don't worry—we'll dive deeper into how Go handles memory in later chapters.

Note If you're new to terms like "garbage collection" or "goroutines," don't worry! These concepts will be explained step by step with practical examples in later chapters.

---

2. Perfect for Cloud-Native Environments

Built for Scalability: In the age of distributed systems, Golang's concurrency model shines. Tools like Kubernetes, Docker, and Istio, all written in Go, leverage its capabilities to scale effortlessly in cloud environments.

Cross-Platform Compatibility: Go makes it easy to build applications that work across various platforms. Its ability to produce static binaries simplifies deployment, especially in containerized environments.

Standard Library for Networking: Go's robust standard library has built-in support for networking and HTTP servers, reducing the need for external dependencies and speeding up development.

3. Simplicity Equals Productivity

Clean and Readable Syntax: Go was designed to reduce cognitive load. With a focus on simplicity, it eliminates features like inheritance and complex metaprogramming, making the code easier to read, write, and maintain.

Short Learning Curve: For enterprises, onboarding new developers can be a challenge. Go's simplicity enables developers, even those new to the language, to become productive quickly.

Minimal Magic: Unlike languages that rely heavily on frameworks and hidden abstractions, Go's philosophy is "what you see is what you get." This predictability makes debugging and optimization straightforward.

4. Cost Efficiency

Fewer Resources, Greater Output: Thanks to Go's efficient use of resources, enterprises can achieve more with fewer servers and reduced operational costs.

Developer Productivity: Go's emphasis on simplicity and tooling ensures that development teams spend less time on debugging and refactoring and more on delivering value.

Open Source Ecosystem: Go's vibrant community and ecosystem mean enterprises can leverage a plethora of high-quality libraries and tools without additional costs.

5. Reliability and Maintainability

Strong Typing: Go uses a system called static typing, which means you must define the type of each variable (like whether it holds a number or text) before you use it. This helps catch errors early and makes your code more reliable. We'll explore Go's type system in later chapters.

Built-In Testing: Go includes a testing framework as part of its standard library, encouraging a test-driven development approach that improves software quality.

Backward Compatibility: Go has committed to backward compatibility in its updates, ensuring that existing codebases remain functional and future-proof.

Use Cases Driving Golang Adoption

1. Microservices Architecture

Golang's lightweight binaries, rapid startup times, and support for gRPC make it an ideal choice for building scalable microservices architectures.

2. DevOps and Infrastructure Tools

The very tools that power DevOps—like Kubernetes, Docker, and Terraform—are written in Go. Enterprises building custom DevOps solutions are naturally drawn to the language.

3. High-Performance APIs

With its low latency and high concurrency capabilities, Go is widely used to build RESTful APIs and high-performance backend services for enterprises.

4. Real-Time Applications

From chat systems to gaming platforms, Golang's concurrency model is well suited for applications requiring real-time processing.

5. Big Data and Stream Processing

For tasks like log aggregation, real-time data processing, and ETL pipelines, Go's speed and scalability make it a strong contender.

Case Studies: Enterprises Betting on Golang

1. Google

As the creator of Go, Google uses it extensively for internal tools and external projects like Kubernetes and gVisor.

2. Uber

Uber migrated many of its core services to Golang, citing its performance and ease of deployment as key advantages.

3. Netflix

Known for their real-time data processing needs, Netflix uses Go for various critical backend services, leveraging its efficiency and concurrency.

4. Dropbox

Dropbox transitioned from Python to Go for performance-critical components, reducing latency and improving scalability.

5. Monzo

This UK-based digital bank built its core banking platform using Go, emphasizing its role in creating scalable and reliable systems.

Your Career with Golang: A World of Opportunities

As enterprises continue to embrace Golang for its performance and simplicity, the demand for skilled Go developers is skyrocketing. Whether you're an aspiring developer, a seasoned professional, or someone looking to pivot to a high-demand field, Golang opens doors to exciting and rewarding career opportunities. Let's explore why building a career in Golang could be more rewarding than pursuing other popular technologies like Python or Java.

1. Golang Career Paths

Golang offers versatile career opportunities across industries and roles. Here are some of the most prominent paths you can pursue:

Backend Developer: Design and build high-performance APIs, microservices, and distributed systems. Contribute to cloud-native applications that are scalable, secure, and efficient.

DevOps Engineer: Work on critical infrastructure tools like Kubernetes, Docker, and Terraform—written in Go. Build CI/CD pipelines, automate deployments, and manage scalable cloud environments.

Systems Engineer: Develop networking tools, proxies, and monitoring systems that handle large-scale traffic and data. Build custom operating systems and kernel modules optimized for performance.

Data Engineer: Create efficient ETL pipelines, data processors, and real-time stream processing applications. Leverage Go's concurrency features to process massive datasets with speed and accuracy.

Open Source Contributor: Join or contribute to major open source projects like Kubernetes, Istio, or Prometheus. Establish yourself as a leader in the thriving Go community.

Freelance Developer: Capitalize on the growing demand for Go developers in startups and enterprises seeking microservices, cloud-native apps, and DevOps solutions.

Emerging Fields

Blockchain: Develop fast and secure blockchain systems, leveraging Go's efficiency.

AI/ML Tooling: Although Go isn't primarily an AI/ML language, its integration capabilities make it a valuable tool for building AI pipelines.

2. Why Golang Is More Rewarding Than Other Technologies

Enterprise-First Design

While Python and Java excel in their respective domains, Golang is purpose-built for modern enterprise needs:

> **Python**: Known for data science and scripting, it lacks the performance and concurrency features required for enterprise-grade backend systems.

> **Java**: While powerful, its verbosity, steep learning curve, and reliance on frameworks make it less productive for quick iterations.

High Demand, Low Supply

As more companies adopt Golang, the talent pool remains limited compared to Python and Java developers. This gap translates to higher salaries and better job security for Go developers. Go's niche appeal means that mastering it can set you apart in the competitive tech job market.

Faster Development Cycles

Golang's simplicity and tooling (e.g., built-in testing, formatting, and linting) lead to faster development cycles, making developers highly productive. This is a critical advantage in enterprise environments where time to market matters.

Cross-Disciplinary Opportunities

Go's ecosystem spans diverse domains, from cloud infrastructure to web services and networking. This breadth allows you to explore and switch domains without changing languages.

Community and Open Source

Go's vibrant and welcoming community offers mentorship, networking, and collaborative opportunities that can accelerate your career growth.

Contributing to high-impact projects like Kubernetes can boost your professional visibility and credibility.

Future-Proofing Your Career

With enterprises moving toward cloud-native, distributed architectures, the demand for Go is projected to grow exponentially.

Unlike older technologies that face gradual decline, Go's growth trajectory is upward, ensuring long-term career relevance.

Conclusion: Your Golang Journey Awaits

Go is more than just a programming language—it's a gateway to building scalable, high-performance applications and an exciting career in modern software development.

Congratulations on taking the first step toward learning Go programming! This book is designed to make your journey enjoyable and rewarding, providing you with the skills to build practical Go applications, including command-line tools and web services.

With Go, you'll discover how simplicity and power come together to create efficient and reliable applications. By the end of this book, you'll have the knowledge and confidence to start building real-world Go projects on your own.

Let's not stop here—turn to *Chapter 1* and start coding your first Go program using Go Playground.

Together, we'll explore the foundations of Go and set the stage for creating useful, impactful applications.

Let Us Go!

CHAPTER 1

Let Us Go on the Playground

1.1 Introduction

Welcome to your journey into Go programming! In this chapter, we will briefly explore the essential features of Go that form the foundation of the language. Through a series of sample programs that you can run on the Go Playground, you will gain a hands-on understanding of Go's syntax and semantics. By the end of this chapter, you will be equipped to write basic Go programs, laying a solid groundwork for more advanced and deep dive topics in the subsequent chapters.

1.2 The Go Playground

The Go Playground is an online tool that allows developers to write, run, and share Go programs in a web browser without needing to set up a local development environment. It provides a safe, sandboxed environment to execute code and supports most of the Go standard library. This tool is invaluable for beginners and professionals alike, offering a quick way to experiment with Go code, debug small snippets, or demonstrate functionality. However, it has limitations, such as no access to the file system or external network connections.

© Rahul Sid Patil 2025
R. S. Patil, *Let Us Go!*, https://doi.org/10.1007/979-8-8688-1442-6_1

The Go Playground is an excellent tool for experimenting with Go code and sharing examples with others.

Try out the Go Playground at https://go.dev/play/.

♀ **Note**   All programs in this chapter can be run on the Go Playground. Just paste the code, click Run, and observe the output.

1.3 Writing and Running Basic Programs

Let's start with a simple "Hello World" program to get a feel for the Go Playground.

1.3.1 Hello World

The "Hello World" program is the starting point for learning any programming language. In Go, it demonstrates the simplicity and structure of the language.

Sample Program:

```
package main

import "fmt"

func main() {
    fmt.Println("Hello, World!")
}
```

Explanation:

- **package main**: Defines the package name. The *main* package is mandatory for building an executable Go program.

- **import "fmt"**: Imports the *fmt* package for formatted I/O operations.

- **func main()**: Declares the *main* function, the entry point of the program.

- **fmt.Println("Hello, World!")**: Calls the *Println* function from the *fmt* package to print the text to the console, followed by a newline.

Output Console:

```
Hello, World!
```

🔗 Try this on Go Playground: https://go.dev/play/.

1.3.2 Values

Values represent immutable data such as *numbers*, *strings*, and *booleans*. They are used to define fixed data in a program and can be used in expressions.

Sample Program:

```go
package main

import "fmt"

func main() {
    fmt.Println("Integer:", 42)
    fmt.Println("Float:", 3.14)
    fmt.Println("String:", "Go is fun!")
    fmt.Println("Boolean:", true)
}
```

Explanation:

- `fmt.Println("Integer:", 42)`: Prints an integer value

- `fmt.Println("Float:", 3.14)`: Prints a floating-point value

- `fmt.Println("String:", "Go is fun!")`: Prints a string value

- `fmt.Println("Boolean:", true)`: Prints a boolean value

Output Console:

```
Integer: 42
Float: 3.14
String: Go is fun!
Boolean: true
```

🔗 Try this on Go Playground: `https://go.dev/play/`.

1.3.3 Variables

Variables in Go store data that can be manipulated during program execution. They are declared using the var keyword or shorthand syntax (:=). Variables can be of primitive types like int, float64, string, or complex types like structs.

a) Short Variable Declaration

The shorthand declaration uses := and is often used inside functions.

Sample Program:

```go
package main

import "fmt"

func main() {
    name := "Alice" // Shorthand declaration
    age := 30       // Type inferred as int
    fmt.Println("Name:", name)
    fmt.Println("Age:", age)
}
```

Explanation:

- **name := "Alice"**: Declares and initializes name with the value "Alice".

- **age := 30**: Declares and initializes age with the value 30. The type is inferred as int.

- **fmt.Println(...)**: Prints the values of name and age.

Output Console:

```
Name: Alice
Age: 30
```

⌘ Try this on Go Playground: https://go.dev/play/.

b) Normal Variable Declaration

The var keyword is used for explicit variable declarations.

Sample Program:

```go
package main

import "fmt"

func main() {
    var score int // Explicitly declares an int variable
    score = 90    // Assigns a value
    fmt.Println("Score:", score)
}
```

Explanation:

- **var score int**: Declares score as an integer variable with an initial value of 0

- **score = 90**: Assigns the value 90 to the variable score

- **fmt.Println("Score:", score)**: Prints the value of score

Output Console:

```
Score: 90
```

🔗 Try this on Go Playground: https://go.dev/play/.

c) Multiple Variable Declaration

Go allows multiple variables to be declared in a single statement.

Sample Program:

```go
package main

import "fmt"

func main() {
    var x, y, z int = 1, 2, 3
    fmt.Println("Values:", x, y, z)
}
```

Explanation:

- **var x, y, z int = 1, 2, 3**: Declares and initializes three variables (x, y, z) of type int

- **fmt.Println(...)**: Prints the values of x, y, and z

Output Console:

```
Values: 1 2 3
```

🔗 Try this on Go Playground: `https://go.dev/play/`.

1.3.4 Constants

Constants represent immutable values that are determined at compile time. They are particularly useful for defining fixed values like `mathematical constants`, `configuration data`, or `enumerations`. In Go, constants can be typed or untyped, offering flexibility in usage.

a) Typed Constants

Typed constants have an explicitly defined type and are constrained by it.

Sample Program:

```go
package main

import "fmt"

func main() {
    const pi float64 = 3.14159 // Typed constant
    const gravity int = 10     // Another typed constant
    fmt.Println("Pi:", pi)
    fmt.Println("Gravity:", gravity)
}
```

Explanation:

- **const pi float64 = 3.14159**: Declares a constant *pi* of type float64

- **const gravity int = 10**: Declares a constant *gravity* of type *int*

- **fmt.Println("Pi:", pi)**: Prints the value of *pi*

- **fmt.Println("Gravity:", gravity)**: Prints the value of *gravity*

Output Console:

```
Pi: 3.14159
Gravity: 10
```

🔗 Try this on Go Playground: https://go.dev/play/.

b) Untyped Constants

Untyped constants are more flexible and adapt to the context in which they are used.

Sample Program:

```
package main

import "fmt"

func main() {
    const x = 42 // Untyped constant
    fmt.Println("x as int:", x+1)
    fmt.Println("x as float:", x+0.5)
}
```

Explanation:

- **const x = 42**: Declares an untyped constant x

- **fmt.Println("x as int:", x+1)**: Uses x as an integer in arithmetic

- **fmt.Println("x as float:", x+0.5)**: Uses x as a floating-point value in arithmetic

Output Console:

```
x as int: 43
x as float: 42.5
```

⊘ Try this on Go Playground: https://go.dev/play/.

c) Enumerated Constants with `iota`

iota is a special identifier used to create sequential values for enumerations in Go. It starts at *0* and increments automatically with each new constant in a block.

Sample Program:

```
package main

import "fmt"

func main() {
    const (
        Sunday = iota // 0
        Monday        // 1
        Tuesday       // 2
    )
    fmt.Println("Days:", Sunday, Monday, Tuesday)
}
```

Explanation:

- **const (Sunday = iota)**: Initializes Sunday with the value 0

- **Monday, Tuesday**: Automatically increments iota to 1 and 2

- **fmt.Println("Days:", Sunday, Monday, Tuesday)**: Prints the values of the constants

Output Console:

```
Days: 0 1 2
```

🔗 Try this on Go Playground: https://go.dev/play/.

1.4 Control Flow

Control flow constructs like for, if/else, and switch are used to determine the order of execution based on conditions or iterations.

1.4.1 For Loop

The for loop is the only looping construct in Go. It can be used in several patterns, including a traditional loop, a while-like loop, and an infinite loop.

a) Traditional **for** Loop

Sample Program:

```
package main

import "fmt"
```

```go
func main() {
for i := 0; i < 5; i++ {
        fmt.Println("Value of i:", i)
    }
}
```

Explanation:

- **for i := 0; i < 5; i++**: Initializes i to 0, runs the loop while i < 5, and increments i by 1 after each iteration

- **fmt.Println("Value of i:", i)**: Prints the value of i during each iteration

Output Console:

```
Value of i: 0
Value of i: 1
Value of i: 2
Value of i: 3
Value of i: 4
```

🔗 Try this on Go Playground: https://go.dev/play/.

b) While-Like **for** Loop

Go's for loop can mimic a while loop by omitting the initialization and increment.

Sample Program:

```go
package main

import "fmt"

func main() {
    i := 0
```

```
    for i < 5 {
        fmt.Println("Value of i:", i)
        i++
    }
}
```

Explanation:

- **i := 0**: Initializes i to 0

- **for i < 5**: Runs the loop while i is less than 5

- **i++**: Increments i by 1 in each iteration

Output Console:

```
Value of i: 0
Value of i: 1
Value of i: 2
Value of i: 3
Value of i: 4
```

🔗 Try this on Go Playground: https://go.dev/play/.

c) Infinite **for** Loop

An infinite loop is created by omitting all three components of the for statement.

Sample Program:

```
package main

import "fmt"

func main() {
    i := 0
```

```
for {
    fmt.Println("Value of i:", i)
    i++
    if i == 5 {
        break
    }
}
}
```

Explanation:

- **for {}**: Declares an infinite loop

- **i++**: Increments i by 1

- **if i == 5 { break }**: Breaks out of the loop when i equals 5

Output Console:

```
Value of i: 0
Value of i: 1
Value of i: 2
Value of i: 3
Value of i: 4
```

🔗 Try this on Go Playground: https://go.dev/play/.

1.4.2 If/Else

The if and else constructs in Go are used for conditional execution. They can also include variable declarations within the condition.

a) Simple If/Else

Sample Program:

```go
package main

import "fmt"

func main() {
    x := 10
    if x > 5 {
        fmt.Println("x is greater than 5")
    } else {
        fmt.Println("x is 5 or less")
    }
}
```

Explanation:

- **if x > 5**: Evaluates whether x is greater than 5

- **fmt.Println("x is greater than 5")**: Executes if the condition is true

- **else { fmt.Println(...) }**: Executes if the condition is false

Output Console:

```
x is greater than 5
```

🔗 Try this on Go Playground: https://go.dev/play/.

1.4.3 Switch

The switch statement in Go is a powerful tool for multi-way branching. It is used to compare a single variable or expression against multiple cases. Unlike some languages, Go's switch does not require explicit break statements to prevent fallthrough. However, you can achieve fallthrough behavior using the fallthrough keyword explicitly.

a) Basic Switch

Sample Program:

```
package main

import "fmt"

func main() {
    day := 3
    switch day {
    case 1:
        fmt.Println("Monday")
    case 2:
        fmt.Println("Tuesday")
    case 3:
        fmt.Println("Wednesday")
    default:
        fmt.Println("Unknown Day")
    }
}
```

Explanation:

- **day := 3**: Declares and initializes a variable day with the value 3

- **switch day**: Evaluates the value of day and matches it to a case

- **case 3:**: Matches the value 3 and executes the associated code block

- **default:**: Executes if no case matches

Output Console:

Wednesday

🔗 Try this on Go Playground: https://go.dev/play/.

1.5 Pointers

Pointers in Go are variables that store the memory address of another variable. They are used to share data between functions without copying it.

1.5.1 Declaring and Using Pointers

Sample Program:

```go
package main

import "fmt"

func main() {
    x := 10
    p := &x // Get the pointer to x
    fmt.Println("Value of x:", x)
    fmt.Println("Pointer p points to value:", *p)
    *p = 20 // Modify x through the pointer
    fmt.Println("Modified value of x:", x)
}
```

Explanation:

- **x := 10**: Declares an integer variable x and assigns it a value of 10

- **p := &x**: Declares a pointer p that stores the address of x

- **fmt.Println("Value of x:", x)**: Prints the value of x

- **fmt.Println("Pointer p points to value:", *p)**: Prints the value pointed to by p, which is x

- ***p = 20**: Modifies the value of x through the pointer p

- **fmt.Println("Modified value of x:", x)**: Prints the modified value of x

Output Console:

```
Value of x: 10
Pointer p points to value: 10
Modified value of x: 20
```

🔗 Try this on Go Playground: https://go.dev/play/.

1.6 Arrays

An array in Go is a fixed-length sequence of elements of the same type. Arrays are used to store multiple values, but their size cannot change after creation. Arrays are used when the size is known and fixed. In most real-world Go programs, slices are preferred due to their flexibility.

1.6.1 Declaring and Using Arrays

Sample Program:

```go
package main

import "fmt"

func main() {
    var numbers [5]int // Declare an array of 5 integers
    numbers[0] = 10    // Assign a value to the first element
    fmt.Println("Array elements:", numbers)
}
```

Explanation:

- **var numbers [5]int**: Declares an array named numbers that can store five integers

- **numbers[0] = 10**: Assigns 10 to the first element of the array

- **fmt.Println("Array elements:", numbers)**: Prints the entire array

Output Console:

```
Array elements: [10 0 0 0 0]
```

🔗 Try this on Go Playground: https://go.dev/play/.

1.7 Slices

Slices are a flexible and more powerful version of arrays. Unlike arrays, slices are dynamically sized and provide convenient methods for manipulating sequences of elements.

1.7.1 Creating and Using Slices

Sample Program:

```
package main

import "fmt"

func main() {
    numbers := []int{1, 2, 3, 4, 5} // Create a slice with
                                     initial values
    fmt.Println("Slice elements:", numbers)
```

```
numbers = append(numbers, 6)     // Append an element to
                                        the slice
fmt.Println("Updated slice:", numbers)
}
```

Explanation:

- **numbers := []int{1, 2, 3, 4, 5}**: Declares and initializes a slice named numbers with five elements

- **fmt.Println("Slice elements:", numbers)**: Prints the slice elements

- **numbers = append(numbers, 6)**: Appends 6 to the slice, expanding its length

Output Console:

```
Slice elements: [1 2 3 4 5]
Updated slice: [1 2 3 4 5 6]
```

🔗 Try this on Go Playground: https://go.dev/play/.

1.8 Maps

Maps in Go are unordered collections of key-value pairs. They are used to implement associative arrays or dictionaries, where each key maps to a specific value.

1.8.1 Declaring and Using Maps

Sample Program:

```
package main

import "fmt"
```

```
func main() {
    capitals := map[string]string{
        "India":     "New Delhi",
        "USA":       "Washington, D.C.",
        "Germany":   "Berlin",
    }
    fmt.Println("Capital of India:", capitals["India"])
}
```

Explanation:

- **capitals := map[string]string{}**: Declares a map named capitals where keys and values are strings

- **fmt.Println("Capital of India:", capitals["India"])**: Prints the value associated with the key "India"

Output Console:

```
Capital of India: New Delhi
```

🔗 Try this on Go Playground: https://go.dev/play/.

1.9 Functions

Functions in Go are a way to encapsulate reusable code. They are defined using the func keyword and can accept parameters and return values.

1.9.1 Declaring and Using Functions

Sample Program:

```
package main

import "fmt"
```

```go
func greet(name string) string {
    return "Hello, " + name
}

func main() {
    message := greet("Alice")
    fmt.Println(message)
}
```

Explanation:

- **func greet(name string) string**: Declares a function named greet that accepts a string parameter and returns a string

- **return "Hello, " + name**: Returns a greeting message with the given name

- **message := greet("Alice")**: Calls the greet function with "Alice" and stores the result in message

Output Console:

```
Hello, Alice
```

🔗 Try this on Go Playground: https://go.dev/play/.

1.10 Multiple Return Values

Go functions can return multiple values, which is useful for functions that need to provide additional information, such as error reporting.

1.10.1 Using Multiple Return Values

Sample Program:

```go
package main

import "fmt"

func divide(a, b int) (int, error) {
    if b == 0 {
        return 0, fmt.Errorf("division by zero")
    }
    return a / b, nil
}

func main() {
    result, err := divide(10, 2)
    if err != nil {
        fmt.Println("Error:", err)
    } else {
        fmt.Println("Result:", result)
    }
}
```

Explanation:

- **func divide(a, b int) (int, error)**: Declares a function named divide that returns an int and an error

- **if b == 0**: Checks if b is zero to avoid division by zero

- **return a / b, nil**: Returns the division result and nil (no error)

- **result, err := divide(10, 2)**: Calls the divide function and handles the result and error

Output Console:

```
Result: 5
```

⏦ Try this on Go Playground: https://go.dev/play/.

1.11 Variadic Functions

Variadic functions in Go accept a variable number of arguments. This is useful when you don't know the exact number of inputs beforehand.

1.11.1 Declaring and Using Variadic Functions

Sample Program:

```go
package main

import "fmt"

func sum(numbers ...int) int {
    total := 0
    for _, number := range numbers {
        total += number
    }
    return total
}

func main() {
    result := sum(1, 2, 3, 4, 5)
    fmt.Println("Sum:", result)
}
```

Explanation:

- **func sum(numbers ...int) int**: Declares a variadic function named sum that accepts any number of int arguments

- **for _, number := range numbers**: Iterates through all the numbers provided

- **total += number**: Adds each number to total

- **result := sum(1, 2, 3, 4, 5)**: Calls the sum function with multiple arguments

Output Console:

```
Sum: 15
```

🔗 Try this on Go Playground: https://go.dev/play/.

1.12 Closures

Closures in Go are functions that reference variables from outside their body. This feature allows functions to capture and use variables even after the surrounding function has returned. Closures are often used to create functions on the fly or to maintain state between function calls.

Sample Program:

```
package main

import "fmt"

func main() {
    adder := func() func(int) int {
        sum := 0
```

```
    return func(x int) int {
        sum += x
        return sum
    }
}

posSum := adder()
fmt.Println(posSum(1)) // 1
fmt.Println(posSum(2)) // 3
fmt.Println(posSum(3)) // 6
}
```

Explanation:

- **adder := func() func(int) int {}**: Declares a function adder that returns another function

- **sum := 0**: Initializes a variable sum to keep track of the total

- **return func(x int) int {}**: Returns an anonymous function that takes an integer x and adds it to sum

- **posSum := adder()**: Creates an instance of the closure

- **posSum(1), posSum(2), posSum(3)**: Invokes the closure, which maintains its own internal state of sum

Output Console:

```
1
3
6
```

🔗 Try this on Go Playground: https://go.dev/play/.

1.13 Recursion

Recursion is a technique in which a function calls itself to solve a problem. In Go, recursion is often used for tasks like calculating factorials or traversing data structures like trees. Care must be taken to ensure a proper base case to avoid infinite recursion.

Sample Program:

```go
package main

import "fmt"

func factorial(n int) int {
    if n == 0 {
        return 1
    }
    return n * factorial(n-1)
}

func main() {
    fmt.Println("Factorial of 5:", factorial(5))
}
```

Explanation:

- **func factorial(n int) int {}**: Declares the recursive function `factorial`.

- **if n == 0 { return 1 }**: Defines the base case; factorial of 0 is 1.

- **return n * factorial(n-1)**: Calls `factorial` recursively with `n-1`.

- **fmt.Println(...)**: Prints the result of `factorial(5)`.

Output Console:

```
Factorial of 5: 120
```

🔗 Try this on Go Playground: https://go.dev/play/.

1.14 Strings and Runes

1.14.1 Strings

Strings in Go are sequences of bytes that represent textual data. Strings are immutable, meaning once created, they cannot be modified. You can use string functions to manipulate and extract information from strings, but any changes will result in the creation of a new string.

Sample Program:

```
package main

import "fmt"

func main() {
    str := "Hello, λ"
    fmt.Println("String:", str)
}
```

Explanation:

- **str := "Hello, λ"**: Declares a string str containing Unicode characters

- **fmt.Println("String:", str)**: Prints the string to the console

Output Console:

```
String: Hello, λ
```

🔗 Try this on Go Playground: https://go.dev/play/.

1.14.2 Runes

Runes in Go represent individual Unicode code points. They are used for handling characters in strings, particularly when dealing with non-ASCII characters. Runes are essential when you need to accurately access and manipulate characters in a string.

Sample Program:

```go
package main

import "fmt"

func main() {
    str := "Hello, λ"
    for i, r := range str {
        fmt.Printf("Index %d: Rune %c\n", i, r)
    }
}
```

Explanation:

- **for i, r := range str**: Iterates over each rune in the string, capturing both the index i and the rune r

- **fmt.Printf("Index %d: Rune %c\n", i, r)**: Prints the index and the rune

Output Console:

```
Index 0: Rune H
Index 1: Rune e
Index 2: Rune l
Index 3: Rune l
Index 4: Rune o
Index 5: Rune ,
```

Index 6: Rune
Index 7: Rune λ

   🔗 Try this on Go Playground: https://go.dev/play/.

1.15 Structs

Structs in Go are composite data types that group together variables under a single name. These variables are called fields, and they can be of different types. Structs are useful for modeling real-world entities and creating more complex data structures.

Sample Program:

```
package main

import "fmt"

type Person struct {
    Name string
    Age  int
}

func main() {
    p := Person{Name: "Alice", Age: 30}
    fmt.Println("Name:", p.Name)
    fmt.Println("Age:", p.Age)
}
```

Explanation:

- **type Person struct {}**: Declares a struct type named Person with two fields, Name and Age

- **p := Person{Name: "Alice", Age: 30}**: Creates an instance of Person named p and initializes the fields

- **fmt.Println("Name:", p.Name)**: Prints the Name field of p

- **fmt.Println("Age:", p.Age)**: Prints the Age field of p

Output Console:

```
Name: Alice
Age: 30
```

🔗 Try this on Go Playground: https://go.dev/play/.

1.16 Methods

Methods in Go are functions that are associated with a specific type. They are a key feature of Go that helps in defining the behavior of types, especially when using structs. Methods allow you to create functions that operate on data of a particular type, similar to how object-oriented programming works.

Sample Program:

```go
package main

import "fmt"

// Define a struct named Rectangle
type Rectangle struct {
    width, height float64
}

// Define a method Area that works on the Rectangle type
func (r Rectangle) Area() float64 {
    return r.width * r.height
}
```

```go
func main() {
    rect := Rectangle{width: 10, height: 5}
    fmt.Println("Area of the rectangle:", rect.Area())
}
```

Explanation:

- **type Rectangle struct {}**: Defines a struct type named Rectangle with two fields, width and height

- **func (r Rectangle) Area() float64 {}**: Declares a method Area that calculates the area of the rectangle

- **rect := Rectangle{width: 10, height: 5}**: Creates an instance of Rectangle

- **rect.Area()**: Calls the Area method on the rect instance

Output Console:

```
Area of the rectangle: 50
```

🔗 Try this on Go Playground: https://go.dev/play/.

1.17 Interfaces

Interfaces in Go provide a way to define the behavior of types. They specify a set of method signatures that a type must implement. Interfaces help in achieving polymorphism and writing more flexible and reusable code.

Sample Program:

```go
package main

import "fmt"
```

```go
// Define an interface named Shape
type Shape interface {
    Area() float64
}

// Define a struct named Circle
type Circle struct {
    radius float64
}

// Implement the Area method for Circle
func (c Circle) Area() float64 {
    return 3.14 * c.radius * c.radius
}

func main() {
    var s Shape
    s = Circle{radius: 5}
    fmt.Println("Area of the circle:", s.Area())
}
```

Explanation:

- **type Shape interface {}**: Defines an interface named Shape with a method Area

- **type Circle struct {}**: Defines a struct named Circle

- **func (c Circle) Area() float64 {}**: Implements the Area method for the Circle type

- **var s Shape**: Declares a variable s of type Shape

- **s = Circle{radius: 5}**: Assigns a Circle instance to s

- **s.Area()**: Calls the Area method on the `Circle`
  instance through the interface

Output Console:

```
Area of the circle: 78.5
```

🔗 Try this on Go Playground: `https://go.dev/play/`.

1.18 Errors

Error handling is an essential part of any programming language, and Go
provides a built-in type error to handle errors. By convention, functions
that may produce an error return an additional error value.

Sample Program:

```
package main

import (
    "errors"
    "fmt"
)

// Define a function that returns an error
func divide(a, b float64) (float64, error) {
    if b == 0 {
        return 0, errors.New("division by zero is not allowed")
    }
    return a / b, nil
}

func main() {
    result, err := divide(10, 0)
```

```
    if err != nil {
        fmt.Println("Error:", err)
    } else {
        fmt.Println("Result:", result)
    }
}
```

Explanation:

- **func divide(a, b float64) (float64, error) {}**: Declares a function divide that returns a float64 and an error

- **if b == 0 {}**: Checks if b is zero to prevent division by zero

- **errors.New("division by zero is not allowed")**: Creates a new error message

- **result, err := divide(10, 0)**: Calls the divide function and handles the error

- **if err != nil {}**: Checks if an error occurred and prints the error message

Output Console:

```
Error: division by zero is not allowed
```

🔗 Try this on Go Playground: https://go.dev/play/.

1.19 Goroutines

Goroutines are lightweight threads managed by the Go runtime. They are a key feature of Go that enables concurrency, allowing you to run functions simultaneously without blocking the main program.

Sample Program:

```go
package main

import (
    "fmt"
    "time"
)

func sayHello() {
    fmt.Println("Hello from Goroutine!")
}

func main() {
    go sayHello() // Start a new goroutine
    fmt.Println("Main function")
    time.Sleep(1 * time.Second) // Wait for the goroutine
                                      to finish
}
```

Explanation:

- **func sayHello() {}**: Defines a function named sayHello

- **go sayHello()**: Starts sayHello as a goroutine

- **time.Sleep(1 * time.Second)**: Pauses the main function to allow the goroutine to complete

Output Console:

```
Main function
Hello from Goroutine!
```

🔗 Try this on Go Playground: https://go.dev/play/.

1.20 Channels

Channels in Go provide a way for goroutines to communicate with each other. Channels can be used to send and receive values between goroutines, making it easier to synchronize their execution.

Sample Program:

```go
package main

import "fmt"

func main() {
    ch := make(chan string)
    go func() {
        ch <- "Hello from channel!" // Send value to channel
    }()
    message := <-ch // Receive value from channel
    fmt.Println(message)
}
```

Explanation:

- **ch := make(chan string)**: Creates a channel of type string. Channels are typed, meaning chan string only allows string values to pass through.

- **go func() { ch <- "Hello from channel!" }()**: Starts a goroutine to send a value to the channel.

- **message := <-ch**: Receives the value from the channel.

- **fmt.Println(message)**: Prints the received value.

Output Console:

```
Hello from channel!
```

🔗 Try this on Go Playground: https://go.dev/play/.

1.21 Select

The select statement in Go allows a goroutine to wait on multiple communication operations. It is useful for handling multiple channels and ensures that the program remains responsive to multiple inputs.

Sample Program:

```
package main

import (
    "fmt"
    "time"
)

func main() {
    ch1 := make(chan string)
    ch2 := make(chan string)

    go func() {
        time.Sleep(1 * time.Second)
        ch1 <- "Message from ch1"
    }()

    go func() {
        time.Sleep(2 * time.Second)
        ch2 <- "Message from ch2"
    }()

    for i := 0; i < 2; i++ {
        select {
        case msg1 := <-ch1:
            fmt.Println(msg1)
```

```
        case msg2 := <-ch2:
            fmt.Println(msg2)
        }
    }
}
```

Explanation:

- **ch1 := make(chan string)**: Creates a channel named ch1

- **ch2 := make(chan string)**: Creates a channel named ch2

- **select {}**: Waits for communication on multiple channels

- **case msg1 := <-ch1:**: Receives a value from ch1 and prints it

- **case msg2 := <-ch2:**: Receives a value from ch2 and prints it

Output Console:

```
Message from ch1
Message from ch2
```

🔗 Try this on Go Playground: https://go.dev/play/.

1.22 Time

The time package in Go provides a rich set of functionalities to work with dates, times, durations, and formatting. It is essential for tasks such as scheduling, timestamping, and measuring elapsed time.

1.22.1 Using the time Package

Sample Program:

```
package main

import (
    "fmt"
    "time"
)

func main() {
    current := time.Now() // Get the current time
    fmt.Println("Current time:", current)

    future := current.Add(2 * time.Hour) // Add 2 hours to the
                                          current time
    fmt.Println("Time after 2 hours:", future)
}
```

Explanation:

- **current := time.Now()**: Gets the current local time

- **fmt.Println("Current time:", current)**: Prints the current time

- **future := current.Add(2 * time.Hour)**: Adds two hours to the current time

- **fmt.Println("Time after 2 hours:", future)**: Prints the updated time

Output Console:

Current time: 2024-11-26 15:04:05.999999999 +0000 UTC m=+0.000000001
Time after 2 hours: 2024-11-26 17:04:05.999999999 +0000 UTC
m=+0.000000001

𝒪 Try this on Go Playground: https://go.dev/play/.

1.23 Reading Files

Reading files is a fundamental part of many applications. In Go, the os
and bufio packages are often used to read data from files. The io/ioutil
package also provides a simple way to read file content.

1.23.1 Reading a File Line by Line

Sample Program:

```go
package main

import (
    "bufio"
    "fmt"
    "os"
)

func main() {
    file, err := os.Open("example.txt")
    if err != nil {
        fmt.Println("Error opening file:", err)
        return
    }
```

```
    defer file.Close()

    scanner := bufio.NewScanner(file)
    for scanner.Scan() {
        fmt.Println(scanner.Text()) // Print each line
    }

    if err := scanner.Err(); err != nil {
        fmt.Println("Error reading file:", err)
    }
}
```

Explanation:

- **file, err := os.Open("example.txt")**: Opens the file named example.txt

- **defer file.Close()**: Ensures the file is closed when the function exits

- **scanner := bufio.NewScanner(file)**: Creates a scanner to read the file line by line

- **for scanner.Scan()**: Iterates over each line in the file

- **fmt.Println(scanner.Text())**: Prints each line

- **if err := scanner.Err(); err != nil**: Checks for errors that occurred during reading

Output Console:

```
<contents of example.txt line by line>
```

1.24 Writing Files

Writing to files is equally important for data persistence. The os package in Go provides functionality to create and write to files.

1.24.1 Writing Text to a File

Sample Program:

```go
package main

import (
    "fmt"
    "os"
)

func main() {
    file, err := os.Create("output.txt")
    if err != nil {
        fmt.Println("Error creating file:", err)
        return
    }
    defer file.Close()

    _, err = file.WriteString("Hello, Go!")
    if err != nil {
        fmt.Println("Error writing to file:", err)
        return
    }

    fmt.Println("File written successfully")
}
```

Explanation:

- **file, err := os.Create("output.txt")**: Creates a new file named output.txt

- **defer file.Close()**: Ensures the file is closed after writing

- **file.WriteString("Hello, Go!")**: Writes the string "Hello, Go!" to the file

- **fmt.Println("File written successfully")**: Prints a success message

Output Console:

```
File written successfully
```

Note   We cannot successfully run file I/O programs on the Go Playground because the Playground is designed as a sandboxed environment for security and simplicity. It does not have access to the local file system, network, or other external resources. As a result, programs that require file system access will fail.

To test this program, you will need to run it locally on your computer. In later chapters, we will guide you on how to set up a Go workspace and an Integrated Development Environment (IDE) to run such programs effectively.

1.25 Testing and Benchmarking

Testing is an integral part of software development. Go provides a built-in testing tool, testing, which allows for unit tests, benchmarks, and example code.

1.25.1 Writing a Unit Test

Sample Program:

File: main.go

```
package main

func Add(a, b int) int {
    return a + b
}
```

File: main_test.go

```
package main

import "testing"

func TestAdd(t *testing.T) {
    result := Add(2, 3)
    expected := 5
    if result != expected {
        t.Errorf("Add(2, 3) = %d; want %d", result, expected)
    }
}
```

Explanation:

- **func TestAdd(t *testing.T)**: Defines a test function for Add. By convention, test functions start with Test.

- **result := Add(2, 3)**: Calls the Add function with 2 and 3.

- **if result != expected**: Checks if the result matches the expected value.

- **t.Errorf(...)**: Reports an error if the result is incorrect.

Output Console:

```
PASS
ok      command-line-arguments      0.001s
```

Note   We can't run this test on the Go Playground because the Playground environment is specifically designed for running simple Go programs and does not support executing tests using the testing package. Additionally, it restricts some runtime features, such as file system access and custom execution commands. Instead, try writing and running this test in your local Go environment after we cover how to set up a Go workspace and an Integrated Development Environment (IDE) in the upcoming chapters.

1.26 Command-Line Arguments

Command-line arguments in Go are used to pass input values when executing a program. They are accessible through the os package, particularly the os.Args variable, which is a slice of strings containing the program name and arguments. Command-line arguments are useful for creating scripts and tools that need external input.

Sample Program:

```go
package main

import (
    "fmt"
    "os"
)
```

```go
func main() {
    args := os.Args // Retrieve command-line arguments
    if len(args) < 2 {
        fmt.Println("Please provide an argument.")
        return
    }
    fmt.Println("Argument received:", args[1])
}
```

Explanation:

- **os.Args**: Retrieves the command-line arguments passed during execution

- **if len(args) < 2**: Checks if the user provided an argument

- **fmt.Println("Argument received:", args[1])**: Prints the first argument passed by the user

Output Console:

```
$ go run main.go Hello
Argument received: Hello
```

Note   We can't run this program successfully on the Go Playground because the Go Playground does not allow passing custom command-line arguments during program execution. It provides a controlled environment for running Go code with fixed input and output, making it unsuitable for programs requiring user-provided arguments. Instead, try writing and running this program in your local Go environment once we cover how to set up a Go workspace and an Integrated Development Environment (IDE) in upcoming chapters.

1.27 HTTP Server

An HTTP server in Go is implemented using the net/http package. Go's standard library makes it easy to set up a basic web server to serve requests and handle routes. It is a fundamental building block for building web services and APIs.

Sample Program:

```
package main

import (
    "fmt"
    "net/http"
)

func handler(w http.ResponseWriter, r *http.Request) {
    fmt.Fprintf(w, "Hello, World!")
}

func main() {
    http.HandleFunc("/", handler) // Register the handler
                                  function for the root URL
    fmt.Println("Starting server on :8080")
    http.ListenAndServe(":8080", nil) // Start the server on
                                      port 8080
}
```

Explanation:

- **http.HandleFunc("/", handler)**: Registers the handler function to handle requests to the root URL

- **handler(w http.ResponseWriter, r *http. Request)**: Defines the function that writes a response to the client

- **http.ListenAndServe(":8080", nil)**: Starts the
  server on port 8080

Output Console:

```
Starting server on :8080
```

Note   We cannot run this program on the Go Playground because
the Playground restricts programs from opening network ports
or accepting external connections for security and resource
management reasons. Instead, try running it locally and then
access http://localhost:8080 in your browser. In later chapters, I
will guide you through setting up a Go workspace and an Integrated
Development Environment (IDE) to make this process easier.

1.28 HTTP Client

An HTTP client in Go allows you to make requests to other servers. The
net/http package provides a convenient way to send GET, POST, and
other HTTP requests. HTTP clients are used for interacting with APIs and
other web resources.

Sample Program:

```
package main

import (
    "fmt"
    "io/ioutil"
    "net/http"
)
```

```go
func main() {
    response, err := http.Get("http://localhost:8080/")
    // Send a GET request
    if err != nil {
        fmt.Println("Error:", err)
        return
    }
    defer response.Body.Close() // Close the response body
                                    when done

    body, _ := ioutil.ReadAll(response.Body) // Read the
                                                response body
    fmt.Println(string(body))
}
```

Explanation:

- **http.Get("https://api.github.com")**: Sends a GET request to the specified URL

- **defer response.Body.Close()**: Ensures that the response body is closed after reading

- **ioutil.ReadAll(response.Body)**: Reads the entire response body

- **fmt.Println(string(body))**: Prints the response body as a string

Output Console:

```
{GitHub API response}
```

Note   We cannot run this program on the Go Playground successfully because it does not allow outgoing or incoming network connections to external servers. This restriction ensures the Playground remains a safe and isolated environment. Instead, try running it locally to access http://localhost:8080. In later chapters, I will guide you through setting up a Go workspace and an Integrated Development Environment (IDE) to make this process easier.

1.29 Context

The context package in Go provides functions to manage deadlines, cancellations, and other request-scoped values across API boundaries. Contexts are especially useful in server-side applications for controlling the life cycle of requests and ensuring that resources are cleaned up appropriately when operations are complete or canceled.

Sample Program:

```
package main

import (
    "context"
    "fmt"
    "time"
)

func main() {
    ctx, cancel := context.WithTimeout(context.Background(),
    2*time.Second)
    defer cancel() // Cancel the context to release resources
```

```go
    select {
    case <-time.After(1 * time.Second):
        fmt.Println("Operation completed")
    case <-ctx.Done():
        fmt.Println("Context timeout:", ctx.Err())
    }
}
```

Explanation:

- **ctx, cancel := context.WithTimeout(context. Background(), 2*time.Second)**: Creates a context with a timeout of two seconds

- **defer cancel()**: Defers the cancel function to release resources when the context is done

- **select {}**: Waits for either the operation to complete or the context to time out

- **<-time.After(1 * time.Second)**: Simulates an operation that takes one second

- **<-ctx.Done()**: Checks if the context has timed out

- **fmt.Println("Context timeout:", ctx.Err())**: Prints an error message if the context times out

Output Console:

```
Operation completed
```

⬦ Try this on Go Playground (https://go.dev/play/) to understand how context can be used to manage timeouts and cancellations effectively.

1.30 Summary

In this chapter, we introduced the fundamentals of the Go programming language, utilizing the Go Playground for a hands-on learning experience. Key topics included core concepts like values, variables, constants, control flow structures, and pointers, providing the groundwork for effective programming in Go. We also ventured into more advanced areas, such as handling command-line arguments, building HTTP servers and clients, and leveraging the context package to manage timeouts and cancellations. Each concept was illustrated with practical examples and detailed explanations, ensuring a solid understanding of Go's syntax and features. This foundational knowledge sets the stage for creating efficient, high-performance applications as you delve deeper into the language.

CHAPTER 2

Setting Up the Go Workspace and VSCode IDE

2.1 Introduction

This chapter provides a detailed, step-by-step guide for setting up the Go programming language workspace and Visual Studio Code (VSCode) IDE on various platforms:

- Windows

- Windows Subsystem for Linux (WSL) Ubuntu 20.04 and above

- Ubuntu 20.04 and above

- macOS

© Rahul Sid Patil 2025
R. S. Patil, *Let Us Go!*, https://doi.org/10.1007/979-8-8688-1442-6_2

Note

- This chapter gives generic instructions about Golang IDE setup on various platforms.

  For specific and up-to-date setup guides and video tutorials, visit `https://github.com/rahulsidpatil/Let-Us-Go-Vol1-artifacts/tree/master/SetUpGuides`.

- Official installation guides may update over time. Always refer to the latest documentation at Go Downloads and VSCode Docs.

2.2 VSCode IDE and Golang Workspace Setup on Windows

2.2.1 Installing Go

1. **Download the Go Installer:**

   - Visit the official Go website: `https://go.dev/dl/`.

   - Download the Windows installer (e.g., `go1.xx.x.windows-amd64.msi`).

2. **Run the Installer:**

   - Locate the downloaded `.msi` file and double-click to run the installer.

   - Follow the on-screen instructions to

     - Accept the license agreement

     - Choose the installation directory (default: `C:\Go`)

3. **Verify Installation:**

   - Open the Command Prompt (cmd) or PowerShell.

   - Run the command:

     go version

   - You should see the installed Go version (e.g., go
     version go1.xx.x windows/amd64).

4. **Set Environment Variables:**

   - Open the **System Properties**:

     - Press Win+Pause/Break, click **Advanced System
       Settings**, then click **Environment Variables**.

   - Add C:\Go\bin to the Path variable in the **System
     Variables** section.

   - Create a new environment variable GOPATH
     with a custom directory path (e.g., C:\
     Users\<YourUsername>\go).

5. **Verify Go Path Setup:**

   - In the terminal, run

     go env

   - Ensure GOPATH and GOROOT are correctly set.

⚠   You do not need to set GOROOT manually unless Go is installed
in a custom location. It defaults to /usr/local/go.

2.2.2 Installing and Setting Up VSCode for Golang Development

1. Download and Install VSCode

- Visit the official VSCode website: `https://code.visualstudio.com/`.

- Download the Windows installer and run it.

- Follow the installation wizard and check the option to add VSCode to the system `Path` for easy command-line access.

2. Install Go Extensions in VSCode

- Launch VSCode after installation.

- Open the Extensions view (`Ctrl+Shift+X`).

- Search for Go and install the **Go extension** by the Go Team at Google.

3. Configure Go in VSCode

- Open VSCode's Command Palette (`Ctrl+Shift+P`).

- Type and select `Go: Install/Update Tools`.

- From the list, install all recommended tools (e.g., `gopls`, `dlv`, `goimports`).

4. Verify Go Setup in VSCode

- Open a terminal in VSCode (`Ctrl+` `` ` ``).

- Run

```
go version
```

- Confirm the Go version displays correctly.

2.2.3 Setting Up a Go Workspace Using VSCode

1. Create a Go Workspace

- Create a directory for your Go workspace (e.g., `C:\`
  `Users\<YourUsername>\go\src\hello_world`).

- Navigate to this directory in VSCode.

2. Initialize a Go Module

- Open the terminal in VSCode and run

```
go mod init hello_world
```

- This command creates a `go.mod` file, initializing
  the module.

3. Write a "Hello World" Program

- In VSCode, create a new file named `main.go` in the
  `hello_world` directory.

- Add the following code:

```
package main

import "fmt"
```

```
func main() {

    fmt.Println("Hello, World!")

}
```

4. Run the Program

- Save the file (Ctrl+S).

- Open the terminal in VSCode and execute

```
go run main.go
```

- You should see the output:

```
Hello, World!
```

Congratulations! You have successfully set up the Go workspace and VSCode IDE for Golang development on Windows. You can now proceed to build more complex programs.

2.3 VSCode IDE and Golang Workspace Setup on WSL Ubuntu

2.3.1 What Is WSL?

WSL (Windows Subsystem for Linux) is a compatibility layer that allows you to run a Linux environment directly on your Windows machine without the need for a virtual machine or dual boot setup. It enables developers to use Linux tools, applications, and workflows seamlessly alongside Windows tools.

2.3.2 How to Enable WSL on Windows

1. **Open PowerShell As Administrator**:

   - Press `Windows+X` and select **Windows PowerShell (Admin)**.

2. **Enable WSL Feature**:

   ```
   dism.exe /online /enable-feature /featurename:
   Microsoft-Windows-Subsystem-Linux /all /norestart
   ```

3. **Enable Virtual Machine Platform (Optional for WSL 2)**:

   ```
   dism.exe /online /enable-feature /featurename:
   VirtualMachinePlatform /all /norestart
   ```

4. **Restart Your Computer**:

   - A restart is required to apply these changes.

5. **Set WSL Version to 2 (Optional)**:

   - Install the WSL 2 kernel update from `https://aka.ms/wsl2kernel`.

   - Set WSL 2 as the default version:

     ```
     wsl --set-default-version 2
     ```

2.3.3 How to Search and Install Ubuntu on WSL

1. **Open Microsoft Store**:

   - Press `Windows+S`, type **Microsoft Store**, and open it.

2. **Search for Ubuntu**:

  • In the search bar, type **Ubuntu**.

3. **Select and Install**:

  • Choose the desired version (e.g., Ubuntu 22.04 LTS) and click **Install**.

4. **Launch Ubuntu**:

  • Once installed, click **Launch** from the Microsoft Store or run `wsl` in PowerShell.

5. **Set Up Ubuntu**:

  • On the first launch, it will ask you to create a username and password. Enter the required details.

2.3.4 How to Configure WSL Ubuntu to Access the Internet Connected to Host PC

1. **Ensure WSL Is Using NAT (Network Address Translation)**:

  • WSL uses the host's internet connection by default. No additional setup is usually required.

2. **Verify Internet Connectivity**:

  • Open your WSL terminal and ping a website:

  ```
  ping google.com
  ```

3. **Troubleshoot If Necessary**:

   - If there is no internet, restart the LxssManager service:

   ```
   net stop LxssManager
   net start LxssManager
   ```

   - Alternatively, restart your computer.

2.3.5 Install Go on WSL Ubuntu

1. **Download the Latest Go Binary**:

   ```
   wget https://go.dev/dl/go1.21.1.linux-amd64.tar.gz
   ```

2. **Extract the Archive to /usr/local**:

   ```
   sudo tar -C /usr/local -xzf go1.21.1.linux-amd64.tar.gz
   ```

3. **Add Go to the PATH Environment Variable**:

   - Open your ~/.bashrc file:

   ```
   nano ~/.bashrc
   ```

   - Add the following lines:

   ```
   export PATH=$PATH:/usr/local/go/bin
   ```

   - Reload the .bashrc file:

   ```
   source ~/.bashrc
   ```

4. **Verify the Installation**:

   ```
   go version
   ```

2.3.6 Install and Set Up VSCode for Golang Development Along with Required Go Extensions on WSL Ubuntu

1. **Download and Install VSCode:**

   - Visit the VSCode download page (`https://code.visualstudio.com/Download`) and install the appropriate version for Windows.

2. **Install the Remote - WSL Extension:**

   - Open VSCode and navigate to the Extensions view (`Ctrl+Shift+X`).

   - Search for **Remote - WSL** and click **Install**.

3. **Open WSL in VSCode:**

   - Press `Ctrl+Shift+P` and type **Remote-WSL: New Window**.

   - This will open a new VSCode window connected to your WSL Ubuntu instance.

4. **Install Go Extension:**

   - In the Extensions view, search for **Go** by the Go Team at Google.

   - Click **Install**.

2.3.7 Set Up Go Workspace Using VSCode, Create, and Execute Hello World Program in the Go Workspace

1. **Create a Go Workspace**:

   - In WSL Ubuntu, navigate to your home directory:

   ```
   cd ~
   ```

   - Create a Go workspace directory:

   ```
   mkdir -p go/src/helloworld
   cd go/src/helloworld
   ```

2. **Initialize a Go Module**:

   ```
   go mod init helloworld
   ```

3. **Write a Hello World Program**:

   - Create a main.go file:

   ```
   nano main.go
   ```

   - Add the following code:

   ```go
   package main

   import "fmt"

   func main() {
       fmt.Println("Hello, World!")
   }
   ```

4. **Open the Project in VSCode:**

   - In the WSL terminal, launch VSCode in the current directory:

   ```
   code .
   ```

5. **Run the Program:**

   - Open the terminal in VSCode (Ctrl+`).

   - Execute the program:

   ```
   go run main.go
   ```

   - You should see

   ```
   Hello, World!
   ```

Congratulations! You have successfully set up the Go workspace and VSCode IDE for Golang development on WSL Ubuntu. You can now proceed to build more complex programs.

2.4 VSCode IDE and Golang Workspace Setup on Ubuntu

This guide provides step-by-step instructions to set up Visual Studio Code (VSCode) and a Golang workspace on Ubuntu for efficient Go development.

2.4.1 Install Go

1. **Update System Packages:**

   ```
   sudo apt update && sudo apt upgrade -y
   ```

2. **Download the Latest Go Version:**

   • Replace <VERSION> with the latest Go version
     (e.g., 1.20):

   ```
   wget https://go.dev/dl/go<VERSION>.linux-
   amd64.tar.gz
   ```

3. **Install Go:**

   • Extract the tarball to /usr/local:

   ```
   sudo tar -C /usr/local -xzf go<VERSION>.linux-
   amd64.tar.gz
   ```

4. **Set Up Environment Variables:**

   • Add the following lines to your ~/.bashrc file:

   ```
   export PATH=$PATH:/usr/local/go/bin
   export GOPATH=$HOME/go
   export PATH=$PATH:$GOPATH/bin
   ```

   • Reload the profile:

   ```
   source ~/.bashrc
   ```

ⓘ If you use Zsh (zsh --version), update ~/.zshrc instead of ~/.bashrc.

---

5. **Verify Installation:**

   • Run the following command to confirm Go is
     installed:

   ```
   go version
   ```

   • You should see output similar to

   ```
   go version go<VERSION> linux/amd64
   ```

2.4.2 Install and Set Up VSCode for Golang Development

1. **Install VSCode:**

   - Add the Microsoft repository:

     ```
     sudo apt install wget gpg -y
     wget -qO- https://packages.microsoft.com/keys/
     microsoft.asc | gpg --dearmor | sudo tee /usr/share/
     keyrings/vscode.gpg > /dev/null
     echo "deb [arch=amd64 signed-by=/usr/share/
     keyrings/vscode.gpg] https://packages.microsoft.
     com/repos/vscode stable main" | sudo tee /etc/apt/
     sources.list.d/vscode.list
     sudo apt update
     sudo apt install code -y
     ```

2. **Launch VSCode:**

   - Open VSCode from the terminal:

     ```
     code
     ```

3. **Install the Go Extension:**

   - Open the Extensions view in VSCode (Ctrl+Shift+X).

   - Search for "Go" and install the official Go extension by golang.go.

4. **Verify Extensions and Tools:**

   - Open the Command Palette (Ctrl+Shift+P) and type Go: Install/Update Tools.

   - Select all recommended tools and click "OK" to install them.

2.4.3 Set Up Go Workspace Using VSCode

1. Create a Workspace Directory

1. Open the terminal and create a directory for your
    Go workspace:

    ```
    mkdir -p ~/go-workspace/src/hello
    cd ~/go-workspace/src/hello
    ```

2. Initialize a Go module in the directory:

    ```
    go mod init hello
    ```

2. Write a "Hello World" Program

1. Create a new file named main.go:

    ```
    nano main.go
    ```

2. Add the following code:

    ```go
    package main

    import "fmt"

    func main() {
        fmt.Println("Hello, World!")
    }
    ```

    *   Save and exit (Ctrl+O, Enter, Ctrl+X).

3. Open Workspace in VSCode

1. Open the `hello` directory in VSCode:

    `code ~/go-workspace/src/hello`

2. You should see the `main.go` file in the Explorer panel.

4. Run the Program

1. Open the integrated terminal in VSCode (Ctrl+`).

2. Run the program:

    `go run main.go`

3. Output:

    `Hello, World!`

By completing these steps, you now have a fully functional Go development environment with VSCode on Ubuntu.

2.5 VSCode IDE and Golang Workspace Setup on macOS

This guide provides a step-by-step walk-through for setting up Visual Studio Code (VSCode) and a Golang workspace on macOS for Go development.

2.5.1 Install Go

1. Download the Go Installer

1. Visit the official Go downloads page: `https://go.dev/dl/`.

2. Download the macOS `.pkg` installer for the latest Go version.

2. Install Go

1. Open the downloaded `.pkg` file.

2. Follow the prompts to complete the installation.

3. Verify Installation

1. Open the Terminal.

2. Run the following command:

    ```
    go version
    ```

3. You should see output similar to

    ```
    go version go<VERSION> darwin/amd64
    ```

4. Set Up Go Environment Variables (Optional)

1. Open your shell configuration file (`~/.zshrc` or `~/.bash_profile`).

2. Add the following lines to set up GOPATH:

    ```
    export GOPATH=$HOME/go
    export PATH=$PATH:/usr/local/go/bin:$GOPATH/bin
    ```

3. Reload the configuration:

```
source ~/.zshrc
```

2.5.2 Install and Set Up VSCode for Golang Development

1. Download and Install VSCode

1. Visit the VSCode website (https://code.visualstudio.com/) and download the macOS version.

2. Open the .dmg file and drag the VSCode app to your Applications folder.

2. Launch VSCode

1. Open VSCode from the Applications folder.

2. Optionally, add VSCode to your PATH for terminal access by running

```
export PATH="$PATH:/Applications/Visual Studio Code.app/Contents/Resources/app/bin"
```

3. Install the Go Extension

1. Open VSCode.

2. Press Cmd+Shift+X to open the Extensions view.

3. Search for "Go" and install the official Go extension by golang.go.

4. Verify Tools Installation

1. Press Cmd+Shift+P to open the Command Palette.

2. Type Go: Install/Update Tools and select it.

3. Select all recommended tools and click "OK" to install them.

2.5.3 Set Up Go Workspace Using VSCode

1. Create a Workspace Directory

1. Open the Terminal.

2. Create a directory for your Go workspace:

   ```
   mkdir -p ~/go-workspace/src/hello
   cd ~/go-workspace/src/hello
   ```

3. Initialize a Go module in the directory:

   ```
   go mod init hello
   ```

2. Write a "Hello World" Program

1. Open the directory in VSCode:

   ```
   code ~/go-workspace/src/hello
   ```

2. Create a new file named main.go with the following content:

   ```
   package main

   import "fmt"
   ```

71

```go
func main() {
    fmt.Println("Hello, World!")
}
```

3. Run the Program

1. Open the integrated terminal in VSCode (Ctrl+`).

2. Run the program:

   ```
   go run main.go
   ```

3. Output:

   ```
   Hello, World!
   ```

By following this guide, you now have a fully functional Go development environment with VSCode on macOS. Happy coding!

2.6 Summary

In this chapter, we covered the step-by-step process of setting up the Go programming environment and the Visual Studio Code (VSCode) IDE on various operating systems, including Windows, WSL Ubuntu, Ubuntu, and macOS. By following the detailed instructions provided, you should now have

- Installed Go and configured the required environment variables (e.g., GOROOT, GOPATH, and PATH) to enable smooth development

- Set up VSCode with the necessary Go extensions and tools for an optimized coding experience

- Created your first Go workspace and successfully executed a "Hello, World!" program to confirm your environment is functional

This foundational setup is crucial for building Go programs efficiently and leveraging the features of a modern development environment like VSCode.

In the next chapter, we will explore source code management by creating and maintaining your own local and remote GitHub repositories. This will equip you with the skills to manage and collaborate on Go projects effectively. Get ready to take your first steps into professional-grade source control!

CHAPTER 3

Setting Up and Maintaining Local and Remote GitHub Repository

3.1 Introduction

In the previous chapter, we explored how to set up the Go workspace and the VSCode IDE, ensuring a productive and efficient development environment tailored for Golang. Now, we turn our attention to one of the most critical tools in a developer's workflow—Git and GitHub.

3.2 Introduction to Git and GitHub

Git and GitHub are powerful tools used by developers worldwide to manage code, collaborate on projects, and track changes efficiently. Understanding these tools is essential for anyone interested in software development or version control.

© Rahul Sid Patil 2025
R. S. Patil, *Let Us Go!*, https://doi.org/10.1007/979-8-8688-1442-6_3

In this chapter, you'll learn how to set up Git on your local machine, create and manage repositories, and use GitHub to collaborate effectively. By the end of this chapter, you'll have a solid understanding of Git and GitHub workflows, preparing you to manage your Golang projects efficiently as we delve deeper into programming concepts in the next chapter.

Note   This chapter gives generic instructions about local and remote GitHub setup on various platforms.

For specific and up-to-date setup guides and video tutorials, visit `https://github.com/rahulsidpatil/Let-Us-Go-Vol1-artifacts/tree/master/SetUpGuides`.

3.2.1 Basics of Version Control

What is a version control system?
A version control system (VCS) is a tool that helps developers manage changes to source code over time. It allows tracking modifications, maintaining a history of changes, and collaborating effectively with team members.

Why do we need a version control system?

- **Collaboration**: Enables multiple developers to work on the same codebase simultaneously without overwriting each other's work

- **History Tracking**: Keeps a detailed log of changes, making it easy to identify when and why a change was made

- **Backup**: Serves as a backup of the project, allowing restoration of previous versions in case of errors or bugs

- **Branching and Merging**: Facilitates experimentation by creating separate branches that can later be merged into the main codebase

- **Conflict Resolution**: Helps resolve conflicts when multiple developers make changes to the same files

Version control systems (VCS) allow developers to track changes to files, collaborate with others, and revert to previous states when necessary. Git is a distributed VCS, which means

- Every user has a complete copy of the repository.

- Changes can be made locally and later synced with remote repositories.

Why Git?

- Tracks changes and logs history

- Allows for branch creation and merging

- Handles collaboration and conflict resolution

Why GitHub?

GitHub is a web-based platform built on top of Git. It provides

- Remote hosting for repositories

- Collaboration tools such as pull requests and issues

- Integration with various development tools and CI/CD pipelines

💬 "You'll use Git to track every change you make to your Go code and collaborate with others when building larger projects."

3.2.2 Setting Up Git on Your Local Machine

To use Git, you need to install it on your computer.

Step 1: Install Git

1. **Windows**

    - Download Git from Git's official website: `https://git-scm.com/`.

    - Run the installer and follow the instructions.

2. **macOS**

    - Use Homebrew: `brew install git`.

3. **Linux**

    - Use your package manager, for example, `sudo apt install git` (Ubuntu/Debian).

Step 2: Configure Git

After installation, configure Git with your user information:

```
# Set your username
$ git config --global user.name "Your Name"

# Set your email
$ git config --global user.email "youremail@example.com"

# Verify your settings
$ git config --list
```

Step 3: Generate an SSH Key (Optional)

SSH keys authenticate your machine with GitHub:

```
# Generate an SSH key
$ ssh-keygen -t rsa -b 4096 -C "youremail@example.com"

# Start the SSH agent
$ eval $(ssh-agent -s)

# Add the SSH key
$ ssh-add ~/.ssh/id_rsa
```

Copy your SSH key and add it to GitHub under **Settings ➤ SSH and GPG keys ➤ New SSH Key**.

3.3 Creating a GitHub Repository

A GitHub repository is a storage location for your project files.

3.3.1 Creating and Cloning Repositories

Step 1: Create a Repository on GitHub

1. Log in to GitHub: `https://github.com/`.

2. Click the **New** button to create a new repository.

3. Provide a repository name and description (optional) and choose visibility (public/private).

4. Initialize the repository with a README (optional) and click **Create repository**.

Step 2: Clone the Repository Locally

Once the repository is created

1. Copy the repository URL.

2. Open your terminal and run

    ```
    # Clone the repository
    $ git clone <repository-url>

    # Navigate into the repository folder
    $ cd <repository-name>
    ```

3.3.2 Committing Changes and Pushing to GitHub

Step 1: Add and Commit Changes

1. Make changes to your project files.

2. Track the changes using

    ```
    # Stage changes
    $ git add .

    # Commit changes
    $ git commit -m "Your commit message"
    ```

Step 2: Push Changes to GitHub

```
# Push to the remote repository
$ git push origin main
```

Replace main with the branch name if you are working on a different branch.

For example, some repositories use master instead of main. If your repo uses master instead of main, use origin master instead.

3.4 Using Git with VSCode

Visual Studio Code (VSCode) integrates seamlessly with Git, providing a graphical interface for version control.

3.4.1 Managing Repositories from VSCode

Step 1: Open a Repository

1. Open VSCode.

2. Go to **File ➤ Open Folder** and select your Git repository.

Step 2: Use the Source Control Panel

1. Click the **Source Control** icon in the Activity Bar.

2. Stage changes by clicking the + icon next to modified files.

3. Add a commit message and click the checkmark icon to commit changes.

Step 3: Push Changes

1. Click the **...** menu in the Source Control panel.

2. Select **Push** to upload changes to GitHub.

3.4.2 Handling Branches and Pull Requests

Step 1: Create and Switch Branches

1. Open the Source Control panel.

2. Click the branch icon in the bottom-left corner.

3. Select **Create new branch**, name your branch, and start working.

Step 2: Merge Branches

1. Push your branch to GitHub.

2. Go to your repository on GitHub and create a pull request.

3. Review the changes and merge the pull request.

Step 3: Resolve Conflicts

1. If there are conflicts, GitHub will notify you.

2. Resolve conflicts in VSCode by editing the files and committing the resolved versions.

3.5 Exercise: Create Your Own GitHub Repository

To reinforce your understanding of Git and GitHub, follow this exercise:

1. **Install Git:**

    - Ensure Git is installed on your local machine. If not, refer to the installation steps in this chapter.

2. **Configure Git**:

- Set your username and email using the following commands:

```
$ git config --global user.name "Your Name"
```

```
$ git config --global user.email "youremail
@example.com"
```

3. **Generate SSH Key**:

- Create an SSH key and link it to your GitHub account. Follow the steps provided in this chapter.

4. **Create a Repository on GitHub**:

- Log in to your GitHub account.

- Click the "New" button and create a repository named "MyFirstRepo."

- Add a description and initialize it with a README file.

5. **Clone the Repository**:

- Copy the repository URL and clone it to your local machine:

```
$ git clone <repository-url>
$ cd MyFirstRepo
```

6. **Add a File**:

- Create a new file named hello.txt and add the following content:

```
Hello, GitHub!
```

- Save the file in the repository folder.

7. **Commit Changes**:

   - Stage and commit the changes:

     ```
     $ git add hello.txt
     $ git commit -m "Added hello.txt"
     ```

8. **Push Changes**:

   - Push the changes to the GitHub repository:

     ```
     $ git push origin main
     ```

9. **Verify on GitHub**:

   - Visit your repository on GitHub to verify that the
     hello.txt file has been successfully uploaded.

Congratulations! You have successfully created your first GitHub repository and performed essential Git operations. This practical experience will serve as a strong foundation as we move forward into programming concepts in the next chapter.

3.6 Summary

This chapter has equipped you with the knowledge and practical steps to

1. Install and configure Git on your local machine across various operating systems

2. Generate SSH keys for secure authentication and link them with your GitHub account

3. Create, clone, and manage repositories on GitHub

4. Use Git commands to add, commit, push, and track changes in your projects

5. Integrate Git with VSCode for a seamless development experience

Mastering these tools ensures a smooth workflow for version control and collaboration. With this foundation, you're now ready to dive into Golang programming concepts and apply them to real-world projects, which we'll explore in the next chapter.

CHAPTER 4

Let Us Go Deep Dive

4.1 Introduction

In this chapter, we will dive deep into the core concepts of the Go
programming language and explore how they come together to enable
efficient, clean, and scalable programming. Go, often praised for its
simplicity and performance, has become a go-to choice for building
modern applications ranging from command-line tools to large-scale
distributed systems.

By understanding these foundational concepts, you will unlock the
potential to create production-grade Go applications that are both robust
and idiomatic. This chapter provides a blend of theory, practical examples,
and exercises to solidify your learning.

Disclaimer   Conceptual explanations throughout this chapter
are based on Go's official documentation, compiler behavior, and
standard language specifications. All examples, exercises, and
wording have been written originally for educational purposes.

© Rahul Sid Patil 2025
R. S. Patil, *Let Us Go!*, https://doi.org/10.1007/979-8-8688-1442-6_4

4.2 Why This Chapter Matters

Whether you're developing a web service, a CLI tool, or a complex distributed system, mastering Go's unique approach to concurrency, memory management, and error handling is essential. Each section in this chapter is designed to

- Introduce a key Go concept with clear explanations

- Provide hands-on examples for immediate application

- Offer exercises to test and reinforce your understanding

4.3 What You'll Learn

By the end of this chapter, you will

1. Grasp Go's primitive and composite data types

2. Work with strings, runes, and textual data

3. Master operators, expressions, and control flow

4. Define and use functions, including Go's multiple return values

5. Explore pointers, structs, and interfaces

6. Harness goroutines and channels for concurrency

7. Implement robust error handling mechanisms

8. Read from and write to files effectively

9. Write unit tests to ensure code correctness

4.4 How to Approach This Chapter

Before diving into the topics, familiarize yourself with some of Go's essential tools, such as go run, go build, and go test. These tools will be your companions as you write, test, and debug your programs. Starting with these tools early will ensure a smoother learning experience and make practicing programming problems more engaging.

4.5 Useful Go Tools

Before we delve into Go's data types, let's explore some of the essential tools provided by the Go ecosystem. These tools are integral to your development workflow and will greatly enhance your productivity. Below, we demonstrate each tool with a practical example and its expected output.

4.5.1 go run

This command compiles and runs a Go program directly.

Example:

```
// File: main.go
package main

import "fmt"

func main() {
    fmt.Println("Hello, Go!")
}
```

Command:

```
go run main.go
```

Output:

```
Hello, Go!
```

4.5.2 go build

This command compiles your Go source code into an executable binary.

Example:

```
// File: main.go
package main

import "fmt"

func main() {
    fmt.Println("This is a compiled Go program.")
}
```

Command:

```
go build main.go
./main
```

Output:

```
This is a compiled Go program.
```

4.5.3 **go test**

This command runs unit tests in your Go project.

Example:

```
// File: main_test.go
package main

import "testing"

func TestAddition(t *testing.T) {
    result := 2 + 2
    if result != 4 {
        t.Errorf("Expected 4, got %d", result)
    }
}
```

Command:

```
go test
```

Output:

```
ok    main    0.001s
```

4.5.4 **go fmt**

This command formats your Go code according to the language's style guidelines.

Example:
Before formatting:

```
package main
import "fmt"
```

```go
func main() {
fmt.Println("Unformatted code")
}
```

Command:

```go
go fmt main.go
```

After formatting:

```go
package main

import "fmt"

func main() {
    fmt.Println("Unformatted code")
}
```

4.5.5 go mod

This command manages dependencies in your Go project.

Example:

```go
go mod init example.com/myproject
```

This creates a go.mod file to manage your project dependencies.

4.5.6 go install

This command downloads and installs executables from source repositories.

Example:

```go
go install github.com/gorilla/mux@latest
```

This installs the mux package at the latest version and places the executable in the Go binary directory ($GOPATH/bin).

Output:

Fetching github.com/gorilla/mux@latest

These tools are essential for writing, testing, and managing Go programs effectively. Familiarizing yourself with their usage will prepare you for the hands-on exercises and examples in this chapter.

Let's begin our journey into the world of Go programming by exploring its data types.

4.6 Data Types

4.6.1 Basic Data Types

int (Integer Types in Go)

What are they?

Go provides several integer types for storing whole numbers, both signed and unsigned, in different sizes:

Type	Description	Size
int	Signed integer, architecture dependent	32- or 64-bit
int8	Signed 8-bit integer	-128 to 127
int16	Signed 16-bit integer	-32,768 to 32,767
int32	Signed 32-bit integer (rune alias)	-2^{31} to $2^{31}-1$
int64	Signed 64-bit integer	-2^{63} to $2^{63}-1$
uint	Unsigned integer, architecture dependent	32- or 64-bit

(continued)

Type	Description	Size
uint8	Unsigned 8-bit integer (byte alias)	0 to 255
uint16	Unsigned 16-bit integer	0 to 65,535
uint32	Unsigned 32-bit integer	0 to 4,294,967,295
uint64	Unsigned 64-bit integer	0 to 18,446,744,073, 709,551,615

Why are they useful?

These types allow precise control over memory and performance.

- Use smaller types like int8 when memory usage is critical.

- Use larger types like int64 for high-range values.

- Use unsigned types when negative numbers are not required.

Where are they used?

- int, uint: General-purpose counters, loops, indices

- int32, int64: Time durations, large IDs, timestamps

- int8, uint8: Byte operations, hardware interfacing

- uint64: File sizes, cryptographic operations

How does the Go Compiler view them?

- int and uint are architecture dependent (32-bit or 64-bit).

- Go enforces strict type safety. You must explicitly convert between different integer types.

- The compiler optimizes integer operations based on system architecture.

Example:

```
package main

import (
    "fmt"
    "unsafe"
)

func main() {
    var a int
    var b int32
    var c uint64
    fmt.Printf("int: %d bytes\n", unsafe.Sizeof(a))
    fmt.Printf("int32: %d bytes\n", unsafe.Sizeof(b))
    fmt.Printf("uint64: %d bytes\n", unsafe.Sizeof(c))
}
```

This program demonstrates how to determine the memory size (in bytes) occupied by various integer types (int, int32, and uint64) using the unsafe package.

Note   The unsafe package in Go is a low-level package that allows you to bypass the Go compiler's type safety and memory safety features. It exposes operations that are not guaranteed to be portable or safe but are sometimes necessary for systems programming or performance-critical code.

- **Programming Exercises:**

    1. Write a program to calculate the sum of the first 100 integers.

    2. Implement a function to find the factorial of a given number using an integer.

float

What is it?

In Go, float refers to data types that represent **real numbers** (i.e., numbers with fractional parts). These are compliant with the **IEEE 754** standard for floating-point arithmetic.

Types of **float** in Go

Go provides two floating-point types:

- float32: Single precision (approximately 6–7 decimal digits)

- float64: Double precision (approximately 15–16 decimal digits)

By default, Go treats floating-point constants and operations as float64 for better precision and range.

⚠ **Note**   Avoid using float for financial calculations due to precision errors. Use big.Float or third-party decimal libraries.

Why is it useful?

Floating-point types are essential when you need to

- Perform calculations involving **decimals** (e.g., measurements, scientific computations)

- Handle **approximations** where exact integers are not sufficient

- Manage **ratios**, **rates**, or **percentages**

Where is it used?

- **Scientific computing** for physical simulations, astronomical models, etc.

- **Graphics and game development** for animation, physics, positioning

- **Financial software** (though often avoided in favor of `decimal` types for accuracy)

- **Machine learning/data science** applications

How does the Go Compiler view it?

- `float64` is the **default** for untyped float constants.

- All operations involving `float32` or `float64` are handled according to **IEEE 754** standards.

- Arithmetic on floats can introduce **rounding errors**, **infinities**, or **NaNs**, so extra care is needed in comparisons and calculations.

- You cannot mix `float32` and `float64` in expressions directly—you must cast explicitly.

Limitations:

- **Precision errors**: `0.1 + 0.2 != 0.3`

- **Not suitable for exact comparisons or financial totals** (use `big.Float` or `decimal` libraries)

Example:

```go
package main

import "fmt"
```

```
func main() {
    var a float32 = 3.14159
    var b float64 = 2.718281828459045

    fmt.Printf("a: %.5f (Type: %T)\n", a, a)
    fmt.Printf("b: %.15f (Type: %T)\n", b, b)
}
```

Output:

```
a: 3.14159 (Type: float32)
b: 2.718281828459045 (Type: float64)
```

This example demonstrates the precision differences and how Go handles each float type.

- **Programming Exercises:**

    1. Write a program to compute the area of a circle given its radius.

    2. Create a function to convert temperatures between Celsius and Fahrenheit.

bool

- **What is it?**

    A bool is a primitive data type in Go that can only hold one of two values: true or false. It is used to represent binary logic or a condition that can either succeed or fail.

- **Why is it useful?**

  Boolean values are the foundation of control flow in programming. They are essential for decision-making constructs (if, switch), loops (for), and binary flags (e.g., isEnabled, hasError). They help express logic clearly and succinctly.

- **Where is it used?**

  bool types are used in

  - if, else, and switch conditions

  - Loop control (for, break, continue)

  - Logical operations (&&, ||, !)

    Function return types to indicate success/failure (ok, found, etc.)

- **How does the Go Compiler view it?**

  The Go compiler treats bool as a distinct type from integers. Unlike in C or Python (where 0 is considered false), Go **does not allow implicit conversion** between integers and booleans. You cannot write if 1—this will result in a compile-time error.

  Internally, a bool is stored as **1 byte** (8 bits) in memory, even though it only needs 1 bit. This simplifies memory alignment and access, which helps optimize performance on modern CPUs. The compiler strictly enforces type safety, which prevents ambiguous logic and makes programs more readable and robust.

- **No implicit conversion from** int **to** bool**:**

```go
// INVALID in Go
if 1 {
    fmt.Println("This won't compile")
}

// VALID
if true {
    fmt.Println("This will compile")
}
```

- **Example:**

```go
package main

import "fmt"

func main() {
    var isActive bool = true
    fmt.Printf("Is Active: %t\n", isActive)

    if isActive {
        fmt.Println("The system is active.")
    } else {
        fmt.Println("The system is inactive.")
    }
}
```

This program demonstrates boolean declaration, its value formatting using %t, and how it controls the execution of conditional blocks.

- **Programming Exercises:**

  1. Implement a program that toggles a boolean value.

  2. Write a function to determine if a given number is even or odd.

strings and runes

📜 What is a String in Go?

- A string in Go is an **immutable sequence of bytes**, typically encoded in **UTF-8**. This means

  - You **can't modify** the contents of a string once it's created.

  - Each character (code point) may occupy **1 to 4 bytes** in memory.

- Internally, a string is represented as a **struct**:

```
type stringStruct struct {
    data *byte // pointer to the start of the
    byte array
    len  int   // length of the byte array (not number
                  of characters)
}
```

So, the memory layout of a string in Go is

- 1 pointer (8 bytes on 64-bit)

- 1 int (8 bytes on 64-bit)

- → **Total: 16 bytes**

Example:

```go
package main

import (
    "fmt"
    "unsafe"
)

func main() {
    s := "Go 💡"
    fmt.Printf("String: %s\n", s)
    fmt.Printf("Length in bytes: %d\n", len(s))
    fmt.Printf("Size of string variable: %d bytes\n", unsafe.Sizeof(s))
}
```

Output:

```
String: Go 💡
Length in bytes: 6
Size of string variable: 16 bytes
```

🔍 The string "Go 💡 " has 6 bytes: "G" (1 byte), "o" (1 byte), and " 💡 " (4 bytes in UTF-8).

What is a Rune in Go?

- A rune is an **alias for** int32 and represents a **single Unicode code point**.

  ```go
  type rune = int32
  ```

- Unlike string, which is a collection of bytes, a rune is just **one character** (which could be up to 4 bytes in UTF-8) stored as a 4-byte integer.

- This makes rune ideal for

    - **Character manipulation**

    - **Unicode handling**

    - Iterating over **multilingual** strings, emojis, and symbols

🎨 String vs. Rune vs. Int

Concept	Type	Memory Size	Represents	Use Case
string	struct	16 bytes	A sequence of UTF-8 encoded bytes	Full text/words/ sentences
rune	int32	4 bytes	A single Unicode code point	Character-level operations
int	Platform dependent (int32 or int64)	4/8 bytes	Whole numbers	Arithmetic, indexing, general-purpose

💡 **Note**   int is typically **64-bit** on 64-bit systems.

🔍 Understanding Rune Iteration in Strings

When using range on a string, Go automatically decodes each UTF-8 code point into a rune.

```
package main

import "fmt"

func main() {
    str := "Go 💡"
```

```
    for i, r := range str {
        fmt.Printf("Index: %d, Rune: %c, Unicode: %U\n", i, r, r)
    }
}
```

Output:

```
Index: 0, Rune: G, Unicode: U+0047
Index: 1, Rune: o, Unicode: U+006F
Index: 2, Rune: 💡, Unicode: U+1F4A1
```

✒ Here, the indices show **byte positions**, not character positions. For accurate character-level operations, always convert string to []rune before indexing.

🧠 **Strings and Runes Internals Recap**

- `string` stores a pointer and length. It does **not store runes** or characters—just raw bytes.

- To manipulate or count **characters**, convert string to a [ ]rune.

```
text := "नमस्ते"
fmt.Println("Byte length:", len(text))
// Output: 18
fmt.Println("Character count:", len([]rune(text)))
// Output: 6
```

- **Programming Exercises:**

    1. Write a program to count the number of unique characters in a string.

    2. Implement a function to convert a string to uppercase using runes.

Interview Questions: Basic Data Types

What?

1. What is the difference between int and int32 in Go?

2. What is a rune, and how does it differ from a byte?

3. What is the default size of the float type in Go?

4. What is the significance of immutability in Go strings?

Why?

1. Why is float64 preferred over float32 in most applications?

2. Why does Go enforce strict type safety for bool values?

3. Why are strings stored as UTF-8 in Go?

4. Why is it important to consider architecture dependency when using int?

How?

1. How does Go handle type conversions between int, float, and string?

2. How can you iterate over runes in a string to process Unicode characters?

3. How does Go ensure memory safety while handling strings?

4. How can you determine the size of a variable of any type at runtime?

What will be the output of this code snippet?

```go
package main

import (
    "fmt"
)

func main() {
    var x int = 5
    var y float64 = 2.5
    // fmt.Println(x + y) // Uncomment this line
}
```

1. What error will this code produce, and how can it be resolved?

   ```go
   package main

   import "fmt"

   func main() {
       str := "GoLang"
       fmt.Printf("Length: %d, First Character: %c\n",
       len(str), str[0])
   }
   ```

2. What will be the output of this code? Explain why.

   ```go
   package main

   import "fmt"

   func main() {
       str := "Hello, 世界"
       for i, r := range str {
   ```

```
        fmt.Printf("Index: %d, Rune: %c, Unicode:
        %U\n", i, r, r)
    }
}
```

3. What does this program demonstrate about indexing and iteration over strings?

    Programming Challenges

    *   Write a program to count the number of vowels in a given string using runes.

    *   Implement a function that takes a slice of integers and returns the maximum value without using built-in functions.

4.6.2 Composite Data Types

Arrays

*   **What is it?**

    An **array** in Go is a **fixed-length**, **homogeneous** collection of elements. All elements in an array are of the same data type, and the length is part of the array's type—for example, [5]int and [10]int are different types.

*   **Why is it useful?**

    Arrays are useful when you know the number of elements at compile time and need predictable, tightly packed memory layout for efficient access. They form the foundation for more complex data structures like slices and matrices.

107

- **Where is it used?**

  Arrays are commonly used in

  - Numeric computations (e.g., 2D matrices, graphs)

  - Fixed-length buffers (e.g., network packet buffers)

  - Lookup tables

  - Embedded or performance-critical systems

- **How does the Go Compiler view it?**

  1. **Memory Layout**

     Arrays are stored in **contiguous blocks of memory**. This ensures

  - **Constant time (O(1)) index-based access**

  - Good CPU cache locality

  - Efficient iteration without pointer chasing

  - For example, the array `[5]int{1, 2, 3, 4, 5}` occupies 5 * `size_of(int)` bytes of contiguous memory. On a 64-bit system, each `int` typically uses 8 bytes, so the total array size is 40 bytes.

  2. **Value Semantics**

  Arrays in Go are **value types**:

  - Assigning one array to another copies all elements.

  - Passing an array to a function passes a copy unless a pointer is used.

    This is unlike slices or pointers which reference shared underlying data.

3. **Strict Bounds Checking**

   Accessing an index outside the array's bounds
   results in a **runtime panic**:

   ```go
   arr := [3]int{1, 2, 3}
   fmt.Println(arr[3]) // panic: index out of range
   ```

4. **Type Safety**

   Arrays of different lengths are considered
   different types:

   ```go
   var a [3]int
   var b [4]int
   // a = b // compile-time error
   ```

- **Example: Array Initialization and Access**

  ```go
  package main

  import "fmt"

  func main() {
      var numbers [5]int = [5]int{1, 2, 3, 4, 5}
      fmt.Println("Numbers:", numbers)

      // Index-based access
      fmt.Println("Third element:", numbers[2])

      // Iterate using for loop
      for i, val := range numbers {
          fmt.Printf("Element at index %d is
          %d\n", i, val)
      }
  }
  ```

- **Visual Representation (Memory Map):**

```
Index:     0    1    2    3    4
Value:     1    2    3    4    5
Address: 0x100 0x108 0x110 0x118 0x120 (assuming 8
bytes per int)
```

Each element lies next to the other in memory,
and the compiler knows the exact byte offset for
each index.

- **Programming Exercises:**

  1. Implement a program to calculate the sum of
      an array.

  2. Write a function to find the maximum element
      in an array.

Slices

- **What is a slice?**

  A **slice** in Go is a flexible, dynamically sized view
  into a sequence of elements stored in an **array**.
  Unlike arrays, slices do not store data themselves—
  they describe a section of an underlying array
  (also known as backing array).

- **Why is it useful?**

  Slices offer powerful abstractions for managing
  sequences of data. They can grow or shrink
  dynamically using functions like append(),
  making them more suitable than arrays for most
  programming tasks.

- **Where is it used?**

  Slices are used extensively in Go programs—for managing lists, buffers, streams of data, dynamic collections, and almost any variable-sized sequence of elements.

- **How does the Go Compiler view a slice?**

  Internally, a slice is represented as a **slice header**, which contains three fields:

  1. **Pointer**: A reference to the first element in the `backing array`

  2. **Length** (`len`): The number of accessible elements in the slice

  3. **Capacity** (`cap`): The maximum number of elements that can be accessed from the pointer (up to the end of the `backing array`)

  Here's how a slice header looks conceptually:

```
type sliceHeader struct {
    Data uintptr  // address of first element in
                        the array
    Len  int      // length of the slice
    Cap  int      // capacity from the starting point
}
```

- **Creating Slices:**

  1. **From an array or another slice:**

```
arr := [5]int{10, 20, 30, 40, 50}
slice := arr[1:4] // slice of arr: {20, 30, 40}
```

2. **Using** make() **function:**

```
slice := make([]int, 3, 5)
fmt.Println(len(slice)) // 3
fmt.Println(cap(slice)) // 5
```

- **Length vs. Capacity:**

  - len(slice): Number of elements the slice
    currently holds

  - cap(slice): Number of elements the slice can hold
    before a new backing array is allocated

- **Example:**

```
s := []int{1, 2, 3}
fmt.Println(len(s)) // 3
fmt.Println(cap(s)) // 3

s = append(s, 4)      // triggers reallocation
fmt.Println(len(s)) // 4
fmt.Println(cap(s)) // >= 4 (typically doubles)
```

- **What is a nil slice?**

  A **nil slice** is a slice with no underlying array (i.e.,
  backing array):

```
var s []int
fmt.Println(s == nil) // true
fmt.Println(len(s))    // 0
fmt.Println(cap(s))    // 0
```

- **Memory Sharing and Mutability:**

  Multiple slices can share the same backing array.
  Modifying the contents of one slice can affect
  the others:

```
arr := [5]int{1, 2, 3, 4, 5}
s1 := arr[1:4]
s2 := arr[2:5]
s1[1] = 99 // changes arr[2], which affects s2[0]
```

- **Example:**

```
package main

import "fmt"

func main() {
    numbers := []int{1, 2, 3, 4, 5}
    fmt.Println("Numbers:", numbers)
    fmt.Printf("len: %d, cap: %d\n", len(numbers),
    cap(numbers))

    numbers = append(numbers, 6)
    fmt.Println("Updated Numbers:", numbers)
    fmt.Printf("len: %d, cap: %d\n", len(numbers),
      cap(numbers))
}
```

- **Output:**

```
Numbers: [1 2 3 4 5]
len: 5, cap: 5
Updated Numbers: [1 2 3 4 5 6]
len: 6, cap: 10
```

In this example, when appending the sixth element, Go allocates a new array (since the old one is full) and copies the contents; hence, capacity increases (commonly doubling in size).

- **Programming Exercises:**

  1. Write a function to remove duplicate elements from a slice.

  2. Create a program to merge two slices into one.

Maps

- **What is it?**

  A map in Go is a built-in data type that stores *unordered* collections of **key-value pairs**. Each key is unique within the map, and accessing a value by its key is extremely fast due to the underlying hash table implementation.

- **Why is it useful?**

  Maps are ideal when you need to associate data in pairs, such as names to phone numbers, user IDs to profile data, or words to definitions. They allow for

  - Constant time average complexity for lookup, insertion, and deletion

  - Flexible use of any comparable type as a key (e.g., int, string, float64, etc.)

- **Where is it used?**

  - Dictionaries or word frequency counters

  - Caching systems (like memoization)

  - Grouping or counting values

  - Storing configurations or settings by name

Deep Dive: Internal Details of Go Maps

- **How does the Go compiler view it?**

  Internally, Go maps are implemented as **hash tables** with a custom structure:

  - A map consists of a **map header** pointing to an array of **buckets**.

  - Each **bucket** contains a group of key-value entries (typically 8).

  - A **hash function** is used to determine which bucket a key belongs to.

  - Go uses **open addressing and overflow buckets** to resolve hash collisions.

- **Map Header Structure (simplified conceptual view):**

```
type hmap struct {
    count       int          // number of key-
                                value pairs
    flags       uint8
    B           uint8        // log_2 of number
                                of buckets
    buckets     *bmap        // pointer to array
                                of buckets
    oldbuckets *bmap         // for map growth
    ...
}
```

  This structure is managed by the Go runtime and isn't directly accessible by users.

115

Creating Maps: make() **vs. Map Literals**

- **Using** make() **Function:**

  ```
  employee := make(map[string]int)
  ```

  This creates a non-nil map ready to use. You can optionally specify an initial capacity:

  ```
  scores := make(map[string]int, 100) // pre-allocates
  space for approx. 100 entries
  ```

  - make() ensures the map is initialized with memory to avoid runtime panics.

  - The optional capacity hint helps optimize memory and avoid reallocation.

- **Using Map Literals:**

  ```
  employee := map[string]int{"Alice": 30, "Bob": 25}
  ```

Convenient for initialization, especially with predefined values.

Map Size and Capacity

- **Length** (len)

  Returns the number of key-value pairs in the map:

  ```
  fmt.Println(len(employee)) // e.g., 2
  ```

- **Capacity** (cap)

  The cap() function does **not** work with maps. Maps grow automatically as needed. Internally, the capacity is managed based on load factor and performance characteristics.

Nil Maps

- A nil map is declared but not initialized:

```
var m map[string]int
```

- It has zero length and can't be written to.

- Reading from it is safe; writing causes a runtime panic:

```
fmt.Println(m["Alice"]) // prints 0
m["Alice"] = 25         // PANIC: assignment to entry
                        //        in nil map
```

Example: Basic Map Usage

```
package main

import "fmt"

func main() {
    // Using map literal
    employee := map[string]int{"Alice": 30, "Bob": 25}
    fmt.Println("Employee Ages:", employee)

    // Using make()
    scores := make(map[string]int)
    scores["Rahul"] = 99
    scores["Priya"] = 87
    fmt.Println("Exam Scores:", scores)

    // Accessing and checking presence
    age, exists := employee["Alice"]
    if exists {
        fmt.Println("Alice's age is", age)
    }
```

```
            // Deleting a key
            delete(employee, "Bob")
            fmt.Println("After deletion:", employee)
        }
```

This program demonstrates

- Creating maps using both literals and the make() function

- Adding and retrieving key-value pairs

- Checking for existence of a key

- Deleting keys from a map

- **Programming Exercises:**

    1. Write a program to count the frequency of words in a string using a map.

    2. Implement a function to find the most frequent key in a map.

Structs

- **What is a struct?**

  A struct is a **composite data type** in Go used to group multiple fields under a single name. Each field can have a different type, making structs a flexible and powerful way to represent structured data.

  ```
  type Person struct {
      Name string
      Age  int
  }
  ```

Why is it useful?

Structs help model **real-world entities** and **custom data formats**. Whether you're building a REST API, managing database records, or defining domain models, structs are foundational in Go.

Where is it used?

- Data modeling (e.g., User, Product, Employee)

- Encapsulating logic via **methods on structs**

- JSON serialization/deserialization

- Database ORM mappings

- Embedded systems where memory layout matters

How does the Go Compiler view structs?

Structs are **value types** in Go:

- Assigning a struct variable to another **copies** the entire struct.

- Passing a struct to a function does the same (unless passed by reference using a pointer).

Go stores struct fields **contiguously in memory**, meaning the order in which fields are defined directly affects

- **Memory alignment**

- **Padding (internal gaps inserted for alignment)**

- **Total size of the struct**

Memory Layout and Field Alignment

Go aligns fields according to their types to optimize memory access speed.

Example:

```
type ExampleA struct {
    A int8  // 1 byte
    B int64 // 8 bytes
    C int8  // 1 byte
}
```

- Without rearrangement, Go introduces padding:

  | A (1B) | padding (7B) | B (8B) | C (1B) | padding (7B) |
  Total = 24B

- Optimized version:

  ```
  type ExampleB struct {
      B int64
      A int8
      C int8
  }
  ```

- Improved layout:

  | B (8B) | A (1B) | C (1B) | padding (6B) | Total = 16B

💡 Always **order fields from largest to smallest** to reduce padding.

Use the unsafe.Sizeof() function to check struct size:

```
fmt.Println(unsafe.Sizeof(ExampleA{})) // Outputs: 24
fmt.Println(unsafe.Sizeof(ExampleB{})) // Outputs: 16
```

Struct Embedding

Go supports **composition over inheritance** using struct embedding.

```
type Address struct {
    City  string
    State string
}

type Employee struct {
    Name    string
    Address // Embedded anonymously
}
```

You can access embedded fields directly:

```
emp := Employee{Name: "Rahul", Address: Address{City: "Pune",
State: "MH"}}
fmt.Println(emp.City) // Pune
```

- Embedded types promote their fields/methods to the outer struct.

- This is Go's way of achieving **"inheritance" through composition**.

Struct Tags

Struct fields can have **tags**—string literals used by libraries (like encoding/json or gorm) for metadata.

```
type User struct {
    ID    int    `json:"id"`
    Name string `json:"name"`
}
```

Use the reflect package to access tags at runtime.

Full Example:

```go
package main

import (
    "fmt"
    "reflect"
    "unsafe"
)

type Address struct {
    City   string
    State string
}

type Person struct {
    Name string `json:"name"`
    Age  int    `json:"age"`
    Address
}

func main() {
    person := Person{Name: "Alice", Age: 30, Address:
    Address{"Pune", "MH"}}
    fmt.Println("Person:", person)
    fmt.Println("Size of Person struct:", unsafe.Sizeof(person))

    t := reflect.TypeOf(person)
    for i := 0; i < t.NumField(); i++ {
        field := t.Field(i)
        fmt.Printf("Field: %s, Tag: %s\n", field.Name,
        field.Tag)
    }
}
```

This program demonstrates

1. **Struct Declaration and Embedding**

   - Defines two structs: Address and Person.

   - Person embeds Address, allowing direct access to its fields (City, State).

2. **Struct Initialization**

   - Creates a Person instance with name "Alice," age 30, and address in Pune, Maharashtra.

3. **Struct Printing**

   - Prints the full Person struct using fmt.Println.

4. **Memory Size Calculation**

   - Uses the unsafe package to print the size (in bytes) of the Person struct.

5. **Reflection and Struct Tags**

   - Uses the reflect package to iterate over the fields of the Person struct.

   - For each field, it prints the **field name** and its associated **struct tag** (like json:"name").

Points to Remember

Feature	Details
Value Type	Copies are made on assignment unless passed by pointer
Memory Layout	Contiguous with possible padding for alignment
Optimization	Order fields by size to reduce struct size
Embedding	Enables reuse and method promotion (composition)
Tags	Metadata used for encoding, validation, etc.

- **Programming Exercises:**

    1. Create a struct to represent a book with fields for title, author, and pages. Write a function to display its details.

    2. Implement a function to calculate the age difference between two Person structs.

Interview Questions: Composite Data Types
What?

    1. What is the difference between arrays and slices in Go?

    2. What are the key components of a slice descriptor?

    3. What is a map in Go, and how is it implemented internally?

    4. What is a struct, and how does it differ from a map?

Why?

    1. Why would you choose a slice over an array in Go?

    2. Why is strict bounds checking important for arrays in Go?

    3. Why is a map preferred over a slice for key-value lookups?

How?

    1. How does the Go compiler handle memory allocation for slices?

    2. How can you dynamically increase the size of an array in Go?

    3. How does Go ensure efficient hash table operations for maps?

What will be the output of this code snippet?

```go
package main

import "fmt"

func main() {
    var arr [3]int
    arr[0], arr[1] = 10, 20
    fmt.Println(arr)
}
```

```go
package main

import "fmt"

func main() {
    slice := []int{1, 2, 3}
    slice = append(slice, 4, 5)
    fmt.Println(slice)
}
```

```go
package main

import "fmt"

func main() {
    m := map[string]int{"a": 1, "b": 2}
    fmt.Println(m["c"])
}
```

```go
package main

import "fmt"

type Person struct {
    Name string
    Age  int
}
```

```go
func main() {
    p1 := Person{Name: "John", Age: 25}
    p2 := p1
    p2.Age = 30
    fmt.Println(p1.Age, p2.Age)
}
```

```go
package main

import "fmt"

func main() {
    slice := []int{1, 2, 3}
    arr := [3]int{1, 2, 3}
    fmt.Println(len(slice), cap(slice))
    fmt.Println(len(arr))
}
```

GitHub Project Demonstrating Data Types

To help you practice and visualize these data types, we have created a
GitHub repository with sample programs:

- **Repository Name**: golang-data-types-demo

- **Repository URL**: https://github.com/
  rahulsidpatil/golang-data-types-demo

The repository contains

- Solutions to programming problems in this section

- Answers to Interview Questions along with explanation

Clone the repository and explore the examples:

```
git clone https://github.com/rahulsidpatil/golang-data-
types-demo.git
```

Summary of Go Data Types

Data Type Category	Description	Examples	Typical Use Cases
int/uint	Whole numbers, signed/unsigned	int, int8, int16, int32, int64, uint, uint8, uint16, uint32, uint64	General arithmetic, counters, indexing
Float	Real numbers (decimals)	float32, float64	Scientific computing, measurements, financials
bool	Logical values	Bool	Conditions, flow control, flags
string	Immutable sequence of bytes (UTF-8)	String	Text processing, I/O, network protocols
rune	Single Unicode code point	rune (alias for int32)	Character manipulation, multilingual text
array	Fixed-size homogeneous collection	[N]Type	Buffers, embedded systems, static data
slice	Dynamic-size view into array	[]Type	Flexible sequences, common in Go programs
map	Unordered key-value store	map[KeyType]ValueType	Dictionaries, lookups, counters
struct	Custom composite type with named fields	struct { Field1 Type1; Field2 Type2; ... }	Models, records, configuration, embedding

4.7 Operators and Expressions

Operators and expressions are the building blocks for performing computations, comparisons, and logical operations in Go. This section provides a detailed look at the types of operators available and how to use them effectively.

4.7.1 Arithmetic Operators

- **What are they?**

  Arithmetic operators are used to perform mathematical operations on numeric values.

- **Why are they useful?**

  They enable basic and complex mathematical computations, which are essential in nearly every programming scenario.

- **Where are they used?**

  They are found in applications ranging from basic calculators to complex data processing.

- **List of Arithmetic Operators:**

  - +: Addition

  - -: Subtraction

  - *: Multiplication

  - /: Division

  - %: Modulus (remainder of division)

- **How does the Go Compiler view them?**

The compiler checks operand types to ensure compatibility (e.g., both operands must be numeric). It performs optimizations for constant expressions during compilation to enhance performance.

Example:

```go
package main

import "fmt"

func main() {
    a, b := 10, 3
    fmt.Printf("Addition: %d\n", a+b)
    fmt.Printf("Subtraction: %d\n", a-b)
    fmt.Printf("Multiplication: %d\n", a*b)
    fmt.Printf("Division: %d\n", a/b)
    fmt.Printf("Modulus: %d\n", a%b)
}
```

This program performs basic arithmetic operations (addition, subtraction, multiplication, division, and modulus) on two integers, 10 and 3, and prints the results.

- **Programming Exercises:**

  1. Write a program to calculate the area of a rectangle given its length and width.

  2. Implement a function to compute the factorial of a number using a loop.

4.7.2 Comparison Operators

- **What are they?**

  Comparison operators are used to compare two values.

- **Why are they useful?**

  They are essential for decision-making in control flow structures like `if` statements and loops.

- **Where are they used?**

  They are commonly used in validating user inputs, implementing search algorithms, and sorting data.

- **List of Comparison Operators:**

  - `==`: Equal to

  - `!=`: Not equal to

  - `<`: Less than

  - `<=`: Less than or equal to

  - `>`: Greater than

  - `>=`: Greater than or equal to

- **How does the Go Compiler view them?**

  The compiler ensures type compatibility between the operands. For example, comparing a string with an integer will result in a compilation error.

Example:

```go
package main

import "fmt"

func main() {
    x, y := 5, 10
    fmt.Println("x == y:", x == y)
    fmt.Println("x != y:", x != y)
    fmt.Println("x < y:", x < y)
    fmt.Println("x <= y:", x <= y)
    fml.Println("x > y:", x > y)
    fmt.Println("x >= y:", x >= y)
}
```

This program compares two integers (x and y) using relational operators (==, !=, <, <=, >, >=) and prints the results of these comparisons.

- **Programming Exercises:**

    1. Write a program to compare two user inputs and print whether they are equal or which one is greater.

    2. Create a function to find the smallest of three numbers.

4.7.3 Logical Operators

- **What are they?**

    Logical operators are used to combine multiple boolean expressions.

- **Why are they useful?**

  They are essential for implementing complex decision-making logic.

- **Where are they used?**

  They are found in validation logic, authentication systems, and conditional flows in applications.

- **List of Logical Operators:**

  - &&: Logical AND

  - ||: Logical OR

  - !: Logical NOT

- **How does the Go Compiler view them?**

  The compiler evaluates logical operators in short-circuit mode, meaning it stops evaluation as soon as the result is determined. For example, in A && B, if A is false, B is not evaluated.

  Example:

```go
package main

import "fmt"

func main() {
    a, b := true, false
    fmt.Println("a && b:", a && b)
    fmt.Println("a || b:", a || b)
    fmt.Println("!a:", !a)
}
```

This program demonstrates the use of basic logical operators (&&, ||, !) by evaluating and printing the results of logical operations between two boolean variables, a and b.

- **Programming Exercises:**

  1. Write a program to validate a user's age for voting eligibility (age >= 18 and age <= 100).

  2. Implement a function to check if a given year is a leap year using logical operators.

Interview Questions: Operators and Expressions
What?

1. What are arithmetic operators, and how do they differ from comparison operators?

2. What is the purpose of the modulus operator, and where can it be practically applied?

3. What is short-circuit evaluation in logical operators?

4. What does it mean when we say operators are "type compatible" in Go?

Why?

1. Why does Go enforce type compatibility for operands in arithmetic and comparison operations?

2. Why is it beneficial for the Go compiler to perform optimizations for constant expressions?

3. Why does short-circuit evaluation improve performance in logical operations?

4. Why is the division operator different for integers and floating-point numbers in Go?

How?

1. How does the Go compiler handle precedence and associativity among multiple operators in an expression?

2. How can logical operators && and || be used to simplify nested if conditions?

3. How can you avoid common pitfalls when using comparison operators on floating-point numbers?

4. How does Go handle division by zero for integers and floating-point numbers?

What will be the output of this code snippet?

```go
package main

import "fmt"

func main() {
    x, y := 10, 3
    fmt.Println("Result:", x / y * y + x % y)
}

package main

import "fmt"

func main() {
    a, b := true, false
    fmt.Println(a && b || !b)
}
```

```
package main

import "fmt"

func main() {
    a := 5
    b := 10
    fmt.Println(a == b || a < b && b > 20)
}
```

GitHub Project Demonstrating Operators and Expressions

To practice and better understand operators and expressions, refer to our GitHub repository:

- **Repository Name**: golang-operators-demo

- **Repository URL**: https://github.com/ rahulsidpatil/golang-operators-demo

The repository includes

- Solutions to programming problems in this section

- Answers to Interview Questions along with explanation

Clone the repository and explore

```
git clone https://github.com/rahulsidpatil/golang-
operators-demo.git
```

4.8 Control Flow

Control flow determines the order in which your program executes statements. Go provides several constructs to manage the flow of execution efficiently. Let's explore them in detail.

4.8.1 Conditional Statements

if and else

- **What is it?**

  The if statement evaluates a condition and executes a block of code if the condition is true. The else statement provides an alternative block of code if the condition is false.

- **Why is it useful?**

  It allows decision-making in programs based on dynamic conditions.

- **Where is it used?**

  It is commonly used in validation checks, input handling, and error detection.

- **How does the Go Compiler view it?**

  The Go compiler requires braces {} for the code blocks, even if they contain a single statement. Unlike some languages, Go does not support parentheses around the condition, enforcing a clean syntax.

  Example:

```go
package main

import "fmt"

func main() {
    age := 18
    if age >= 18 {
        fmt.Println("You are eligible to vote.")
```

```
    } else {
        fmt.Println("You are not eligible to vote.")
    }
}
```

This program checks if the variable age is 18 or
older and prints "You are eligible to vote." if true;
otherwise, it prints "You are not eligible to vote."

- **Programming Exercises:**

  1. Write a program to determine if a given number
     is positive, negative, or zero.

  2. Implement a program that checks if a year is a
     leap year.

switch

- **What is it?**

  The switch statement is a concise way to test a
  variable against multiple values.

- **Why is it useful?**

  It simplifies branching logic compared to multiple
  if-else statements.

- **Where is it used?**

  It is often used in menus, state management, and
  handling specific cases.

- **How does the Go Compiler view it?**

  Go's switch is more flexible than many other languages. Cases do not fall through by default, eliminating the need for break statements. You can also use expressions in cases.

  Example:

```go
package main

import "fmt"

func main() {
    day := "Monday"
    switch day {
    case "Monday", "Tuesday", "Wednesday":
        fmt.Println("It's a weekday.")
    case "Saturday", "Sunday":
        fmt.Println("It's the weekend.")
    default:
        fmt.Println("Invalid day.")
    }
}
```

  This program determines whether a given day is a weekday, a weekend, or invalid and prints the corresponding message.

- **Programming Exercises:**

  1. Write a program to display the name of a month based on its number.

  2. Implement a menu-driven program for basic arithmetic operations.

4.8.2 Loops

Overview

Go provides **only one looping construct**, for, but this versatile keyword can be used in multiple forms to achieve behavior similar to while, do-while, and traditional for loops from other languages.

Loops are used to perform repetitive tasks such as iterating through collections, repeating computations, or processing input/output until a condition is met.

1. Traditional **for** Loop (like C-Style)

What is it?

A three-part loop: initialization, condition check, and post-statement. This is equivalent to the classic for loop found in C/C++/Java.

Syntax:

```
for initialization; condition; post {
    // loop body
}
```

Example:

```
for i := 0; i < 5; i++ {
    fmt.Println("i:", i)
}
```

When to use it?

When you know in advance how many times to iterate (count-controlled loops).

2. Condition-Only for Loop (like while)

What is it?

A for loop that acts like a while loop by omitting the initialization and post-statements.

Syntax:

```
i := 0
for i < 5 {
    fmt.Println("i:", i)
    i++
}
```

When to use it?

When the number of iterations depends on a condition being met.

3. Infinite for Loop

What is it?

A for loop with no condition, making it an infinite loop unless broken manually with a break statement or a return.

Syntax:

```
for {
    // loop body
}
```

Example:

```
for {
    fmt.Println("Running forever...")
    break // or return, or use condition inside
}
```

When to use it?

For event-driven programs, servers, retry logic, or polling loops.

4. for...range Loop

What is it?

A specialized form of for used to iterate over slices, arrays, maps, strings, and channels.

Syntax:

```
for index, value := range collection {
    // loop body
}
```

Example:

```
nums := []int{10, 20, 30}
for idx, val := range nums {
    fmt.Printf("Index: %d, Value: %d\n", idx, val)
}
```

When to use it?

When traversing collections (like slices, maps, etc.) in a clean, readable way.

Compiler Perspective

Go's for loop is highly optimized by the compiler. Because there is only one loop construct, it simplifies code generation and avoids unnecessary abstraction. The range keyword compiles into efficient internal loops, and map iteration uses safe hashing mechanisms.

When to Use Which Loop

Variant	When to Use
`for init; condition; post`	Fixed iteration count
`for condition`	Loop until a condition is false
`for {}`	Infinite loops (break manually)
`for range`	Iterating collections

Programming Exercises

Using traditional `for` loop:

1. Write a program to calculate the factorial of a number.

2. Generate a multiplication table for any number.

Using condition-only `for`:

1. Write a program to reverse a number (e.g., input: 1234 → output: 4321).

2. Simulate a login retry system that allows three attempts.

Using infinite `for`:

1. Build a program that keeps reading user input until the word "exit" is typed.

2. Create a countdown timer (in seconds) that terminates with a message.

Using `for...range`:

1. Calculate the sum of all elements in a slice.

2. Display all keys and values in a map.

3. Iterate over a string and print each character and its Unicode code point.

4. Count the frequency of each character in a string.

4.8.3 Defer, Panic, and Recover

In Go, defer, panic, and recover are control flow mechanisms used to manage execution, error handling, and cleanup in an elegant and idiomatic way.

defer

- **What is it?**

    defer postpones the execution of a function call until the surrounding function completes (returns or panics).

- **Why is it useful?**

    It helps in resource cleanup: closing files, unlocking mutexes (mutex is a lock mechanism used to synchronize access to shared resources), rolling back transactions, etc.

- **How does the Go compiler handle it?**

    Deferred calls are pushed onto a stack and executed in **LIFO** (Last-In-First-Out) order when the function exits.

- **Common use cases:**

    - File or network connection cleanup

    - Unlocking a mutex

- Logging function entry/exit

- Error recovery with recover

Example:

```
package main

import "fmt"

func main() {
    defer fmt.Println("Deferred: This prints last.")
    fmt.Println("This prints first.")
}
```

Output:

```
This prints first.
Deferred: This prints last.
```

Multiple defer calls:

```
func example() {
    defer fmt.Println("third")
    defer fmt.Println("second")
    defer fmt.Println("first")
}
```

Output:

```
first
second
third
```

panic

- **What is it?**

  panic abruptly stops the flow of execution and begins **stack unwinding** (i.e., executing all deferred functions).

- **Why is it useful?**

  It's used for handling **unrecoverable conditions**, such as

  - Invalid memory access

  - Nil pointer dereference

  - Critical initialization failure

- **Where to use:**

  Only in exceptional situations. Avoid panics in normal logic flow.

  Example:

```
func mayPanic() {
    panic("Critical failure!")
}
```

recover

- **What is it?**

  recover is a built-in function used **inside a deferred function** to catch a panic and regain control.

- **Why is it useful?**

  It prevents a program from crashing and enables graceful shutdown or custom error logging.

  Example:

```
func safeCall() {
    defer func() {
        if r := recover(); r != nil {
            fmt.Println("Recovered from:", r)
        }
    }()

    panic("Something went wrong!")
}
```

🛠 Programming Exercises

1. **Defer and Resource Cleanup**

   Write a function that opens a file, reads content, and ensures the file is closed using defer.

2. **Panic Simulation**

   Write a program that performs a division operation. Trigger panic when dividing by zero.

3. **Recover from Panic**

   Extend the above program to recover from a panic and print a friendly error message.

Interview Questions: Control Flow
What?

1. What is the purpose of the if statement in Go?

2. What is the significance of the defer keyword in Go, and how does it manage execution flow?

3. What is a `switch` statement, and how does it differ from `if-else` constructs in Go?

4. What is the only looping construct in Go, and how can it replace `while` loops?

5. What does the `range` keyword do in a loop, and what types does it support?

Why?

1. Why does Go enforce braces {} for conditional and loop code blocks?

2. Why does the `switch` statement in Go not require `break` statements by default?

3. Why is the `recover` function useful when dealing with `panic` in Go?

4. Why does Go provide only one looping construct (`for`) instead of multiple options like `while` and `do-while`?

5. Why is `defer` important for resource management in Go?

How?

1. How can you use a `for` loop in Go to iterate through a slice of integers?

2. How does the `recover` function help in handling panics in a Go application?

3. How do you implement a `switch` statement in Go to handle multiple related cases with a single code block?

4. How do you calculate the sum of all elements in a slice using the range keyword?

5. How does Go's for loop handle infinite loops, and how can you implement one?

What will be the output of this code snippet?

```go
package main

import "fmt"

func main() {
    age := 20
    if age >= 18 {
        fmt.Println("Eligible to vote")
    } else {
        fmt.Println("Not eligible to vote")
    }
}
```

```go
package main

import "fmt"

func main() {
    day := "Monday"
    switch day {
    case "Monday", "Tuesday":
        fmt.Println("Start of the week")
    case "Saturday", "Sunday":
        fmt.Println("Weekend")
    default:
        fmt.Println("Midweek")
    }
}
```

```go
package main

import "fmt"

func main() {
    for i := 0; i < 3; i++ {
        defer fmt.Println(i)
    }
}
```

```go
package main

import "fmt"

func main() {
    numbers := []int{1, 2, 3, 4}
    sum := 0
    for _, num := range numbers {
        sum += num
    }
    fmt.Println("Sum:", sum)
}
```

```go
package main

import "fmt"

func main() {
    defer func() {
        if r := recover(); r != nil {
            fmt.Println("Recovered from panic:", r)
        }
    }()
    panic("Unexpected error!")
}
```

GitHub Project Demonstrating Control Flow Concepts

- **Repository Name**: golang-control-flow-demo

- **Repository URL**: https://github.com/
  rahulsidpatil/golang-control-flow-demo

The repository contains

- Solutions to programming problems in this section

- Answers to Interview Questions along with explanation

Clone the repository and explore the examples:

```
git clone https://github.com/rahulsidpatil/golang-control-
flow-demo.git
```

4.9 Functions

4.9.1 Function Declaration and Calling

- **What is it?**

  A function in Go is a named, reusable block of code
  designed to perform a specific task.

- **Why is it useful?**

  Functions promote **code reuse**, **separation of
  concerns**, and **testability**. They allow you to write
  cleaner and modular programs.

- **Where is it used?**

  Functions are used everywhere—from utility logic
  and business rules to orchestrating workflows in
  web servers and CLI tools.

- **How does the Go Compiler view it?**

  In Go, functions are **first-class citizens**. This means

  - They can be assigned to variables.

  - They can be passed as arguments to other functions.

  - They can be returned from other functions.

  ```go
  package main

  import "fmt"

  func greet() {
      fmt.Println("Hello, World!")
  }

  func main() {
      greet()
  }
  ```

- **Programming Exercises:**

  1. Write a function that prints "Welcome to Go programming!"

  2. Implement a function to calculate the square of a number.

  3. Create a function that takes your name as input and prints "Hello, !"

4.9.2 Parameters and Return Values

- **What are they?**

  Parameters allow data input into a function. Return values allow the function to send results back.

- **Variants in Go:**

  - **Multiple parameters**

  - **Named vs. unnamed return values**

  - **Multiple return values**

- **Named vs. Unnamed Returns:**

```
// Unnamed return value
func multiply(a, b int) int {
    return a * b
}

// Named return value
func divide(a, b float64) (result float64) {
    result = a / b
    return // implicit return
}
```

- **Use Cases:**

  - Named returns are useful for documentation and readability.

  - Multiple return values are useful for returning results and error information together.

- **How does the Go Compiler handle them?**

  The compiler ensures **strict type matching** and validates return values at compile time.

- **Programming Exercises:**

  1. Create a function that returns the minimum and maximum of two integers.

  2. Write a function that calculates and returns both area and perimeter of a rectangle.

4.9.3 Variadic Functions

- **What is it?**

  A variadic function can accept **zero or more** values of a specified type.

- **Why is it useful?**

  It helps in processing arbitrary-length inputs without requiring a slice.

- **Example:**

```
func sum(nums ...int) int {
    total := 0
    for _, n := range nums {
        total += n
    }
    return total
}
```

- **How does the Go Compiler handle it?**

  The variadic parameter is treated as a slice internally (...int becomes []int).

- **Programming Exercises:**

  1. Create a variadic function that joins multiple strings using a separator.

  2. Write a variadic function that finds the average of given float64 numbers.

4.9.4 Anonymous Functions and Closures

- **What are they?**

  - **Anonymous Functions**: Functions without names

  - **Closures**: Anonymous functions that capture variables from the surrounding scope

- **Why are they useful?**

  Useful for encapsulating logic locally, creating callbacks, or writing function factories.

- **Example:**

```go
func main() {
    // Anonymous function
    double := func(n int) int {
        return n * 2
    }
    fmt.Println(double(5)) // Output: 10

    // Closure with captured variable
    counter := func() func() int {
        count := 0
        return func() int {
            count++
            return count
        }
    }()
    fmt.Println(counter()) // 1
    fmt.Println(counter()) // 2
}
```

- **Programming Exercises:**

  1. Define a closure that keeps a running total (accumulator).

  2. Implement an inline function to reverse a slice of integers.

4.9.5 Function Variables and Higher-Order Functions

- **What are they?**

  - Functions can be stored in variables.

  - Functions can accept other functions as arguments or return them.

- **Use Cases:**

  - Creating pipelines

  - Implementing strategies or function composition

  - Event dispatchers and middleware patterns

- **Example:**

```go
func apply(op func(int, int) int, a, b int) int {
    return op(a, b)
}

func main() {
    add := func(x, y int) int { return x + y }
    fmt.Println("Result:", apply(add, 10, 5))
}
```

- **Programming Exercises:**

  1. Write a function that takes another function and a slice of integers and applies the function to each element.

  2. Implement a chain of functions that transforms a string using multiple function variables.

4.9.6 Recursion

- **What is it?**

  A function calling itself is recursion.

- **Use Case:**

  Useful for tasks that can be broken into smaller subproblems: factorial, Fibonacci, tree traversal.

- **Example:**

```
func factorial(n int) int {
    if n == 0 {
        return 1
    }
    return n * factorial(n-1)
}
```

- **Programming Exercises:**

  1. Implement a recursive Fibonacci generator.

  2. Write a recursive function to calculate the sum of digits of a number.

☑ Summary

Feature	Description
Named Return Values	Improve readability; useful for documentation
Variadic Functions	Allow passing a flexible number of arguments
Anonymous Functions	Useful for short-lived operations or closures
Closures	Allow functions to remember surrounding state
Function Variables	Enable function passing, returning, and reuse
Recursion	Useful for divide-and-conquer problems

Interview Questions: Functions
What?

1. What is the primary purpose of a function in programming?

2. What are variadic functions in Go, and how do they differ from regular functions?

3. What is a closure, and how does it work in Go?

Why?

1. Why are functions considered the building blocks of modular programming?

2. Why is it beneficial for Go to allow multiple return values from a function?

3. Why are closures useful in programming, particularly in Go?

How?

1. How does Go ensure type safety in function parameters and return values?

2. How do variadic functions collect and manage their arguments in Go?

3. How can anonymous functions be used to handle events or callbacks in Go?

What will be the output of this code snippet?

```go
package main

import "fmt"

func multiply(a, b int) int {
    return a * b
}

func main() {
    result := multiply(3, 4)
    fmt.Println("Result:", result)
}

package main

import "fmt"

func main() {
    greet := func(name string) string {
        return "Hello, " + name
    }
    fmt.Println(greet("Rahul"))
}
```

```go
package main

import "fmt"

func counter() func() int {
    count := 0
    return func() int {
        count++
        return count
    }
}

func main() {
    increment := counter()
    fmt.Println(increment())
    fmt.Println(increment())
    fmt.Println(increment())
}

package main

import "fmt"

func sum(numbers ...int) int {
    total := 0
    for _, num := range numbers {
        total += num
    }
    return total
}

func main() {
    fmt.Println("Sum:", sum(1, 2, 3))
    fmt.Println("Sum:", sum())
}
```

GitHub Project Demonstrating Functions

To help you practice and visualize these function-related concepts, we have created a GitHub repository with sample programs:

- **Repository Name**: `golang-functions-demo`

- **Repository URL**: `https://github.com/ rahulsidpatil/golang-functions-demo`

The repository contains

- Solutions to programming problems in this section

- Answers to Interview Questions along with explanation

Clone the repository and explore the examples:

```
git clone https://github.com/rahulsidpatil/golang-
functions-demo.git
```

4.10 Pointers in Go

4.10.1 Understanding Pointers

What is a pointer?

A **pointer** is a variable that holds the **memory address** of another variable. In Go, pointers are **type-safe**—a pointer to an int cannot be used as a pointer to a float64.

```
var x int = 10
var p *int = &x // p stores the address of x
```

Why are pointers useful?

- They **avoid copying** large data structures.

- They allow **modifying values** directly via reference.

- They help implement **linked lists, trees, and other complex data structures**.

- They make **functions more efficient** by working on memory references.

Where are pointers used?

- When updating a variable inside a function

- When sharing a common resource (like a struct) among multiple functions

- When working with **interfaces**, **slices**, **maps**, and **channels** (some of which use internal pointers)

Go Compiler's View

- Go restricts unsafe pointer arithmetic.

- Pointer dereferencing is safe and well checked.

- The compiler uses **escape analysis** to determine if a variable should be on the heap or stack.

Example

```
package main

import "fmt"

func main() {
    var x int = 10
    var ptr *int = &x
    fml.Prinlf("Value of x: %d, Address of x: %p\n", x, ptr)
}
```

Programming Exercises

1. Write a function to **swap two integers** using pointers.

2. Create a function to **double the value** of an integer using a pointer.

3. Print the **address and value** of multiple variable types using pointers.

4.10.2 Pointer Variants and Operations

Pointer Declaration and Initialization

```
var p *int      // Declared but not initialized (nil)
p = new(int)    // Allocates memory and returns pointer
*p = 100        // Dereference and assign
```

Nil Pointer

- A pointer that points to **no valid memory address**.

- Dereferencing a `nil` pointer causes a **runtime panic**.

  ```
  var p *int
  fmt.Println(p) // Output: <nil>
  ```

Dangling Pointer

- Go's garbage collector **prevents** traditional dangling pointers seen in C/C++.

- However, referencing a freed object via unsafe code (e.g., `unsafe.Pointer`) **may simulate** it—**avoid**.

Pointer Arithmetic

- Go **does not support** pointer arithmetic.

- This reduces the chance of memory corruption.

Example: Dereferencing

```
var a int = 42
var p *int = &a
fmt.Println(*p) // 42
```

Programming Exercises

1. Use new() to allocate and initialize an integer pointer.

2. Show how modifying a pointer value changes the original variable.

3. Write a function that safely checks for nil before dereferencing a pointer.

4.10.3 Pointers in Functions

Passing Pointers to Functions

- Enables **in-place updates** to variables

- Saves memory for large structs/slices

```
func update(num *int) {
    *num = *num + 10
}
```

Compiler Notes

- Automatically handles pointer dereferencing

- Tracks **escape scope** and ensures memory safety

Example

```
func updateValue(num *int) {
    *num = 50
}
```

Programming Exercises

1. Write a function that **updates multiple values** via pointers.

2. Pass a pointer to a **custom struct** and update a field.

3. Build a function that accepts a pointer to a string and appends text to it.

4.10.4 Pointers with Arrays, Slices, and Maps

Arrays and Pointers

- In Go, **arrays are value types**. When passed to a function, a copy of the array is made.

- This means that any modification made to the array inside the function **won't affect** the original array unless a pointer to the array is passed.

- To **avoid copying** and **enable modification** of the original array, you can pass a pointer to the array.

```go
func modifyArray(arr *[3]int) {
    (*arr)[0] = 100
}

func main() {
    a := [3]int{1, 2, 3}
    modifyArray(&a)
    fmt.Println(a) // Output: [100 2 3]
}
```

Slices and Pointers

- Slices in Go are built-in **reference types.** Internally, a slice has three components: a pointer to the underlying array, the length, and the capacity.

- When you pass a slice to a function, the **pointer to the underlying array is copied**, so modifications made to slice elements inside the function **are visible** to the caller.

- However, if you **re-slice or append** inside the function, it may point to a new array, and changes may not reflect outside.

```
func modifySlice(s []int) {
    s[0] = 99           // This modifies the
                           original array
    s = append(s, 4)   // This does not affect the
                           original slice
}

func main() {
    a := []int{1, 2, 3}
    modifySlice(a)
    fmt.Println(a) // Output: [99 2 3]
}
```

Maps and Pointers

- Maps in Go are also **reference types.** When a map is passed to a function, changes made to its contents **are reflected** in the caller.

- You don't need to pass a pointer to a map to update it, because the map variable already contains a reference to the underlying data.

- However, if you reassign the map inside the function (e.g., m = make(map[string]int)), it won't affect the original.

```
func updateMap(m map[string]int) {
    m["key"] = 100 // This updates the original map
}
func main() {
    m := map[string]int{"key": 0}
    updateMap(m)
    fmt.Println(m) // Output: map[key:100]
}
```

Summary Table

Type	Passed by	Reference?	In-Place Modifications	Notes
Array	Value	✘	Only via pointer	Full copy on pass
Slice	Value	☑	Yes (underlying array)	Re-slicing may affect copy
Map	Value	☑	Yes	Reference type

Programming Exercises

1. Pass a pointer to an array and modify its elements.

2. Pass a slice to a function and modify it—verify that element updates persist, but appends may not.

3. Create a function that updates values in a map passed as an argument.

4. Write a function that appends to a slice inside a function and returns the modified slice.

5. Compare the memory address of slice elements before and after appending in a function to understand reallocation.

4.10.5 Summary of Pointer Types in Go

Pointer Type	Description
*int	Pointer to int
*string	Pointer to string
*struct	Pointer to a custom struct
nil pointer	Zero-value pointer (not initialized)
Pointer to array	Used for entire array modifications
Pointer to interface	Requires type assertions (rare use)

Programming Challenges

1. **Swap two numbers** using pointers.

2. **Implement a linked list node** structure using struct pointers.

3. **Create and modify a matrix** (2D array) using pointer-to-array.

4. **Write a function** that receives a slice and doubles each element.

5. **Demonstrate memory safety**: safely check for nil and handle errors.

Interview Questions: Pointers
What?

1. What is a pointer, and how is it represented in Go?

2. What is the difference between a `nil` pointer and an uninitialized pointer in Go?

3. What is the purpose of the & and * operators in pointer manipulation?

Why?

1. Why does Go disallow pointer arithmetic, unlike C or C++?

2. Why would you use pointers instead of passing variables by value in a Go program?

3. Why is dereferencing a `nil` pointer unsafe, and how can you avoid it in Go?

How?

1. How do you declare a pointer to a struct in Go, and how can you access its fields?

2. How can pointers improve the efficiency of passing large data structures to functions?

3. How can you safely initialize and use pointers in a concurrent Go program?

Code Output

1. What will be the output of the following code snippet, and why?

```
package main

import "fmt"
```

```go
func main() {
    var a int = 20
    var p *int
    p = &a
    fmt.Println(*p)
    *p = 50
    fmt.Println(a)
}
```

2. What will happen if you try to dereference a `nil` pointer in Go? Demonstrate with an example.

3. What will be the output of the following code, and why?

```go
package main

import "fmt"

func modifyValue(ptr *int) {
    *ptr = 100
}

func main() {
    val := 10
    fmt.Println("Before:", val)
    modifyValue(&val)
    fmt.Println("After:", val)
}
```

Mixed

4. What happens if you pass a pointer to a slice to a function in Go? How does it differ from passing the slice itself?

5. Why might you use a pointer receiver in a method instead of a value receiver? Provide a practical example.

6. How would you handle a `nil` pointer error gracefully in a Go program? Provide a code example.

GitHub Project Demonstrating Pointers

To help you practice and visualize pointers, we have created a GitHub repository with sample programs:

- **Repository Name**: `golang-pointers-demo`

- **Repository URL**: `https://github.com/ rahulsidpatil/golang-pointers-demo`

The repository contains

- Solutions to programming problems in this section

- Answers to Interview Questions along with explanation

Clone the repository and explore the examples:

```
git clone https://github.com/rahulsidpatil/golang-
pointers-demo.git
```

4.11 Structs and Methods

4.11.1 Defining Structs

- **What is it?**

  A `struct` is a composite data type that groups together fields, each with its own type, under a single entity.

- **Why is it useful?**

  Structs enable you to model real-world entities and manage related data more effectively.

- **Where is it used?**

  Structs are widely used in scenarios requiring structured data representation, such as APIs, database models, and application configurations.

- **How does the Go Compiler view it?**

  Structs are value types, meaning assignments create a copy. The compiler lays out struct fields in contiguous memory locations to optimize access. Padding and alignment are handled to meet platform-specific requirements, which can impact memory usage and performance.

  Example:

```
package main

import "fmt"

type Person struct {
    Name string
    Age  int
}

func main() {
    person := Person{Name: "Alice", Age: 30}
    fmt.Printf("Person: %+v\n", person)
}
```

  This program defines a struct Person and initializes it with values.

- **Programming Exercises:**

    1. Define a struct to represent a Car with fields for Make, Model, and Year. Write a function to display the car's details.

    2. Create a struct to represent a Rectangle. Add fields for Length and Width, and calculate its area.

4.11.2 Methods on Structs

- **What are they?**

    Methods are functions associated with a struct type, enabling behaviors specific to that type.

- **Why are they useful?**

    Methods allow encapsulating functionality and data, making code more modular and intuitive.

- **Where are they used?**

    They are commonly used to implement object-oriented patterns, such as encapsulation and polymorphism.

- **How does the Go Compiler view them?**

    Methods are syntactic sugar for functions with a receiver parameter. The compiler resolves method calls by associating them with the receiver's type. Receiver parameters can be values or pointers, influencing performance and mutability.

Example:

```go
package main

import "fmt"

type Rectangle struct {
    Length, Width float64
}

func (r Rectangle) Area() float64 {
    return r.Length * r.Width
}

func main() {
    rect := Rectangle{Length: 5, Width: 3}
    fmt.Printf("Area: %.2f\n", rect.Area())
}
```

This code demonstrates a method Area defined on the Rectangle struct.

- **Programming Exercises:**

  1. Add a method to the Car struct to calculate its age based on the current year.

  2. Implement methods for the Rectangle struct to calculate perimeter and check if it is a square.

4.11.3 Pointer Receivers vs. Value Receivers

- **What are they?**

  Methods can use either pointer or value receivers to access the struct fields.

- **Why are they useful?**

  Pointer receivers allow modifying the original struct, while value receivers work on copies.

- **Where are they used?**

  Use pointer receivers for methods that modify the struct or are computationally expensive due to copying large data.

- **How does the Go Compiler view them?**

  The compiler optimizes method calls based on the receiver type. Pointer receivers enable in-place modifications, reducing memory overhead for large structs, while value receivers ensure immutability.

  Example:

```go
package main

import "fmt"

type Counter struct {
    Count int
}

func (c *Counter) Increment() {
    c.Count++
}
```

```go
func (c Counter) Display() {
    fmt.Println("Count:", c.Count)
}

func main() {
    counter := Counter{Count: 0}
    counter.Increment()
    counter.Display()
}
```

This example shows how pointer and value receivers are used for different purposes.

- **Programming Exercises:**

    1. Implement a BankAccount struct with methods for deposit, withdraw, and displaying the balance. Use pointer receivers for deposit and withdraw.

    2. Create a Circle struct with methods to calculate area and circumference. Use value receivers.

Interview Questions: Structs and Methods
What?

1. What is a struct in Go, and how does it differ from other data types?

2. What are the advantages of using methods with structs?

3. What is the difference between pointer and value receivers in Go methods?

Why?

1. Why does Go prefer structs over classes in
    its design?

2. Why would you choose a pointer receiver over a
    value receiver for a method?

3. Why is it important to understand the memory
    layout of a struct?

How?

1. How does the Go compiler optimize the use of
    structs in memory?

2. How can you initialize a struct with values in
    different ways?

3. How can you associate multiple methods with a
    single struct?

Code Snippet Questions

1. What will be the output of the following code
    snippet, and why?

    ```go
    package main

    import "fmt"

    type Test struct {
        Value int
    }

    func (t Test) UpdateValue(v int) {
        t.Value = v
    }
    ```

```go
func main() {
    t := Test{Value: 5}
    t.UpdateValue(10)
    fmt.Println(t.Value)
}
```

2. What will be the output of this code snippet? Explain
    the behavior.

```go
package main

import "fmt"

type Counter struct {
    Count int
}

func (c *Counter) Increment() {
    c.Count++
}

func main() {
    counter := Counter{Count: 1}
    counter.Increment()
    fmt.Println(counter.Count)
}
```

3. What will happen if you change the Increment
    method in the above example to use a value
    receiver? Explain.

4. What will be the output of the following code,
    and why?

```go
package main

import "fmt"

type Point struct {
    X, Y int
}

func (p Point) Translate(dx, dy int) {
    p.X += dx
    p.Y += dy
}

func main() {
    pt := Point{X: 0, Y: 0}
    pt.Translate(5, 10)
    fmt.Printf("Point: (%d, %d)\n", pt.X, pt.Y)
}
```

Practical Scenarios

5. How would you design a struct and associated
    methods to represent a student record system?

6. How can you ensure that a struct is immutable after
    its creation?

7. How can you extend the functionality of structs
    using methods without introducing performance
    bottlenecks?

Miscellaneous

8. Why are structs in Go considered more lightweight than objects in object-oriented programming languages?

9. What are some best practices to follow while designing and using structs in Go?

GitHub Project Demonstrating Structs and Methods

To help you practice and understand structs and methods, we have created a GitHub repository with sample programs:

- **Repository Name**: `golang-structs-methods-demo`

- **Repository URL**: `https://github.com/rahulsidpatil/golang-structs-methods-demo`

The repository contains

- Solutions to programming problems in this section

- Answers to Interview Questions along with explanation

Clone the repository and explore the examples:

```
git clone https://github.com/rahulsidpatil/golang-structs-methods-demo.git
```

4.12 Interfaces in Go

Interfaces are a cornerstone of Go's type system and support powerful design principles like abstraction, decoupling, and polymorphism—without the need for inheritance.

4.12.1 Defining and Implementing Interfaces

- **What is an interface?**

  An **interface** in Go defines a set of method signatures (a *contract*) that any type can implement implicitly. Unlike other languages, Go uses **structural typing**, meaning a type satisfies an interface just by implementing its methods—**no need to explicitly declare that a type implements an interface**.

- **Why are interfaces useful?**

  - Promote **decoupling** of code and logic (e.g., use behavior without worrying about the concrete type).

  - Enable **polymorphism**: functions can operate on multiple types as long as they implement the same interface.

  - Enhance **testability**: you can mock implementations by using interfaces.

  - Support clean and scalable **API design** by separating what is done from how it is done.

- **Syntax (Declaring an Interface):**

```go
type Reader interface {
    Read(p []byte) (n int, err error)
}
```

- **Compiler Representation:**

  Internally, an interface value in Go is represented as

```
type iface struct {
    tab  *itab              // Pointer to type
                               information and
                               method table
    data unsafe.Pointer  // Pointer to actual
                               concrete data
}
```

  This enables **dynamic dispatch**, meaning Go decides which method implementation to call **at runtime**.

Example: Implementing an Interface in Steps

Let's understand how to use an interface with a simple example step by step.

Step 1: Define an Interface

```
type Shape interface {
    Area() float64
}
```

Here, Shape is an interface that expects any type to have a method called Area() that returns a float64.

Step 2: Create a Struct Type

```
type Circle struct {
    Radius float64
}
```

This is a concrete type. We'll now make it implement the Shape interface.

Step 3: Implement the Interface Method

```go
func (c Circle) Area() float64 {
    return 3.14 * c.Radius * c.Radius
}
```

Now, Circle implements the Shape interface because it has a method Area() with the expected signature.

Step 4: Write a Function That Accepts the Interface

```go
func printArea(s Shape) {
    fmt.Println("Area:", s.Area())
}
```

This function takes any Shape and prints its area.

Step 5: Put It All Together

```go
package main

import "fmt"

type Shape interface {
    Area() float64
}

type Circle struct {
    Radius float64
}

func (c Circle) Area() float64 {
    return 3.14 * c.Radius * c.Radius
}

func printArea(s Shape) {
    fmt.Println("Area:", s.Area())
}
```

```
func main() {
    c := Circle{Radius: 5}
    printArea(c) // Circle satisfies the Shape interface
}
```

Sample Output:

```
Area: 78.5
```

This demonstrates how interfaces let us **write generic functions** that work across different types implementing the same behavior. We could add Rectangle, Triangle, etc., and reuse the same printArea() function.

4.12.2 Types of Interfaces in Go

Go provides different kinds of interfaces to model a variety of behavior. Understanding these types helps you build modular and extensible programs. Below are the common interface types with explanations and examples.

Type	Description
Regular Interface	Interface with one or more method signatures that types must implement
Empty Interface (interface{})	Interface that can hold any type, used for generic behavior or unknown types
Composite Interface	Combines multiple interfaces into one using interface embedding
Interface with Embedding	Embeds other interfaces to extend or reuse behaviors

1. Regular Interface

Explanation: A regular interface contains one or more method signatures. Any type implementing those methods satisfies the interface.

```
package main

import "fmt"

type Speaker interface {
    Speak() string
}

type Dog struct{}

func (d Dog) Speak() string {
    return "Woof!"
}

func main() {
    var s Speaker = Dog{}
    fmt.Println(s.Speak())
}
```

Output:

```
Woof!
```

2. Empty Interface (`interface{}`)

Explanation: The empty interface can hold values of any type. It's useful when the type is not known in advance.

```
package main

import "fmt"
```

```go
func describe(i interface{}) {
    fmt.Printf("Type: %T, Value: %v\n", i, i)
}

func main() {
    describe(42)
    describe("hello")
}
```

Output:

```
Type: int, Value: 42
Type: string, Value: hello
```

3. Composite Interface

Explanation: A composite interface combines multiple interfaces into one. A type that satisfies all embedded interfaces satisfies the composite interface.

```go
package main

import "fmt"

type Reader interface {
    Read(p []byte) (n int, err error)
}

type Writer interface {
    Write(p []byte) (n int, err error)
}

type ReadWriter interface {
    Reader
    Writer
}
```

```go
type File struct{}

func (f File) Read(p []byte) (int, error) {
    fmt.Println("Reading data")
    return len(p), nil
}

func (f File) Write(p []byte) (int, error) {
    fmt.Println("Writing data")
    return len(p), nil
}

func main() {
    var rw ReadWriter = File{}
    rw.Read([]byte("sample"))
    rw.Write([]byte("sample"))
}
```

Output:

```
Reading data
Writing data
```

4. Interface with Embedding

Explanation: Interfaces can embed other interfaces, reusing their methods and extending them with more functionality.

```go
package main

import "fmt"

type Animal interface {
    Move() string
}
```

```go
type Mammal interface {
    Animal
    Feed() string
}

type Human struct{}

func (h Human) Move() string {
    return "Walks on two legs"
}

func (h Human) Feed() string {
    return "Eats food"
}

func main() {
    var m Mammal = Human{}
    fmt.Println(m.Move())
    fmt.Println(m.Feed())
}
```

Output:

```
Walks on two legs
Eats food
```

4.12.3 Interface As Function Parameters and Return Types

Interfaces are frequently used to

- Accept a **range of types** in a single function
- Return **behavior** instead of concrete data types

This is especially useful when designing functions or APIs that work with a variety of types that share common behavior.

📖 Explanation

Imagine you are creating a program to calculate the area of different shapes. Each shape (like Circle, Rectangle, Triangle) has a different formula for calculating area. But we want to write **one function** that can accept any of these shapes and call their Area() method.

That's where **interfaces** help. You can define a Shape interface with an Area() method and write a generic function like printArea() that accepts any type that satisfies the Shape interface.

☑ Code Example

```go
package main

import "fmt"

// Step 1: Define the interface

type Shape interface {
    Area() float64
}

// Step 2: Define concrete types that implement the interface

type Circle struct {
    Radius float64
}

func (c Circle) Area() float64 {
    return 3.14 * c.Radius * c.Radius
}

type Rectangle struct {
    Width, Height float64
}
```

```go
func (r Rectangle) Area() float64 {
    return r.Width * r.Height
}

// Step 3: Accept interface as function parameter

func printArea(s Shape) {
    fmt.Printf("The area is: %.2f\n", s.Area())
}

// Step 4: Return an interface type from a function

func NewCircle(radius float64) Shape {
    return Circle{Radius: radius}
}

func NewRectangle(width, height float64) Shape {
    return Rectangle{Width: width, Height: height}
}

func main() {
    c := NewCircle(5)
    r := NewRectangle(4, 3)

    printArea(c)
    printArea(r)
}
```

Sample Output

```
The area is: 78.50
The area is: 12.00
```

🎨 Summary

- **Interface As Parameter**: Use when a function should accept different types that follow the same behavior.

- **Interface As Return Value**: Use when you want to hide the exact type and just return a behavior.

This pattern makes your code more **extensible**, **testable**, and **clean**, especially in large applications.

4.12.4 Empty Interface and Type Assertion

- **What is it?**

  The interface{} is known as the **empty interface** in Go. It doesn't specify any methods, which means **every type in Go implements it by default**. This makes it the most flexible type and allows you to **store any value**—integers, strings, structs, slices, maps, functions, and even other interfaces.

- **Beginner-Friendly Explanation:**

  Think of interface{} as a box where you can put anything inside, but once it's in, you don't know what exactly is in the box until you open it. To use what's inside, you need to **check its type**.

- **Why is it useful?**

  - Acts like a **generic container**

  - Used when the function doesn't know what exact type it will receive

- Commonly used in

  - fmt.Println() to print values of any type

  - JSON marshalling/unmarshalling (encoding/json package)

  - map[string]interface{} to store dynamic data like configuration

☑ **Example 1: Assigning Different Types to an Empty Interface**

```
package main

import "fmt"

func main() {
    var i interface{}

    i = 42
    fmt.Println("Integer value:", i)

    i = "Hello, Go!"
    fmt.Println("String value:", i)

    i = []int{1, 2, 3}
    fmt.Println("Slice value:", i)
}
```

Output:

```
Integer value: 42
String value: Hello, Go!
Slice value: [1 2 3]
```

⚒ **Extracting Values from an Empty Interface**

To use the original value, you must extract it using **type assertion** or **type switch**.

Example 2: Type Assertion

```go
package main

import "fmt"

func main() {
    var val interface{} = "hello"

    str, ok := val.(string)
    if ok {
        fmt.Println("It's a string:", str)
    } else {
        fmt.Println("Type assertion failed")
    }
}
```

Output:

```
It's a string: hello
```

Example 3: Type Switch

```go
package main

import "fmt"

func describe(i interface{}) {
    switch v := i.(type) {
    case int:
        fmt.Println("Integer:", v)
    case string:
        fmt.Println("String:", v)
    case []int:
        fmt.Println("Slice of ints:", v)
```

```
    default:
        fmt.Println("Unknown type")
    }
}

func main() {
    describe(42)
    describe("hello")
    describe([]int{1, 2, 3})
}
```

Output:

```
Integer: 42
String: hello
Slice of ints: [1 2 3]
```

☑ Using type switches and assertions correctly helps you write **safe and flexible code** when dealing with unknown types.

🚫 Avoid using `interface{}` everywhere unless it's necessary. It defeats the purpose of type safety and makes your code harder to maintain.

4.12.5 Reflection with Interfaces

Go's `reflect` package allows you to inspect and manipulate variables at runtime—even if you don't know their exact types during compilation.

This is useful in cases like

- Debugging or logging generic data

- Writing serialization/deserialization logic (e.g., encoding/json)

- Building frameworks or tools that work with arbitrary types

---

⚠ **Caution**   Reflection should be used sparingly. It bypasses compile-time checks and is generally slower and less safe than regular code.

Beginner-Friendly Explanation

Imagine you have a variable of type interface{}—you don't know what's inside it. With reflect, you can ask questions like

- What type is this?

- What is its value?

Let's see this in action.

Example: Print Type and Value

```
package main

import (
    "fmt"
    "reflect"
)
```

```go
func printTypeAndValue(i interface{}) {
    t := reflect.TypeOf(i)
    v := reflect.ValueOf(i)
    fmt.Printf("Type: %s, Value: %v\n", t, v)
}

func main() {
    printTypeAndValue(42)
    printTypeAndValue("hello")
    printTypeAndValue([]string{"Go", "Rust", "Python"})
}
```

Sample Output:

```
Type: int, Value: 42
Type: string, Value: hello
Type: []string, Value: [Go Rust Python]
```

Example: Detecting Pointer or Struct

```go
package main

import (
    "fmt"
    "reflect"
)

type User struct {
    Name string
    Age  int
}

func inspect(i interface{}) {
    val := reflect.ValueOf(i)
    typ := reflect.TypeOf(i)
```

```go
    if typ.Kind() == reflect.Ptr {
        fmt.Println("It's a pointer to:", typ.Elem())
    } else {
        fmt.Println("It's a value of type:", typ)
    }

    fmt.Println("Fields and values:")
    for i := 0; i < val.NumField(); i++ {
        field := val.Type().Field(i)
        value := val.Field(i)
        fmt.Printf("  %s: %v\n", field.Name, value)
    }
}

func main() {
    u := User{Name: "Rahul", Age: 35}
    inspect(u)
}
```

Sample Output:

```
It's a value of type: main.User
Fields and values:
  Name: Rahul
  Age: 35
```

Reflection gives you dynamic access to data types, fields, and values. It's powerful but should be used judiciously.

4.12.6 Interface Internals: Memory Model

To understand how interfaces work in Go, it's helpful to peek under the hood.

- **What happens when you assign a concrete type to an interface?**

  When a value is assigned to an interface, Go stores two things:

  - type: Metadata about the actual type (e.g., Circle)

  - data: A pointer to the actual data/value (e.g., a Circle with radius 5.0)

  Together, this pair forms what is known as an **interface value**.

```go
package main

import "fmt"

type Shape interface {
    Area() float64
}

type Circle struct {
    Radius float64
}

func (c Circle) Area() float64 {
    return 3.14 * c.Radius * c.Radius
}

func describe(i Shape) {
    fmt.Printf("Type: %T\n", i)
    // prints the dynamic type
    fmt.Printf("Value: %v\n", i)
    // prints the dynamic value
    fmt.Printf("Area: %.2f\n", i.Area())
    // uses the method
}
```

```
func main() {
    var s Shape = Circle{Radius: 5}
    describe(s)
}
```

- **Sample Output:**

```
Type: main.Circle
Value: {5}
Area: 78.50
```

- In the example above

  - s is of interface type Shape, but it holds a value of concrete type Circle.

  - Internally, Go tracks

    - Type: main.Circle

    - Data: Pointer to Circle{Radius: 5}

- **Equality in Interfaces**

  Two interface values are considered **equal** if

  1.   Their **dynamic types** are the same.

  2.   Their **underlying values** are equal.

```
func main() {
    var a Shape = Circle{Radius: 5}
    var b Shape = Circle{Radius: 5}
    fmt.Println("a == b:", a == b)
}
```

- **Sample Output:**

```
a == b: true
```

However, this will print false if their dynamic types differ—even if their values look the same.

```
type MyCircle Circle // distinct type

func main() {
    var a Shape = Circle{Radius: 5}
    var b Shape = MyCircle{Radius: 5} // different dynamic type

    fmt.Println("a == b:", a == b)
}
```

Sample Output:

```
a == b: false
```

Understanding this memory model helps in debugging interface-related bugs and designing APIs that use interfaces effectively.

4.12.7 Interface Design Patterns in Go

Go interfaces enable clean, maintainable code by allowing you to implement classic design patterns in a simple and idiomatic way. Here are some common patterns explained in beginner-friendly terms with examples and expected output:

1. **Strategy Pattern**

   - **What is it?**

     A pattern that allows switching between different algorithms (strategies) at runtime without changing the code that uses them.

   - **When to use?**

     When you want to support multiple algorithms that can be interchanged easily.

- **Example:**

```go
package main

import "fmt"

type CompressionStrategy interface {
    Compress(data string) string
}

type ZipCompression struct{}
func (z ZipCompression) Compress(data string) string {
    return "ZIP: " + data
}

type TarCompression struct{}
func (t TarCompression) Compress(data string) string {
    return "TAR: " + data
}

func compressData(data string, strategy
CompressionStrategy) {
    fmt.Println(strategy.Compress(data))
}

func main() {
    compressData("myfile.txt", ZipCompression{})
    compressData("myfile.txt", TarCompression{})
}
```

- **Output:**

ZIP: myfile.txt

TAR: myfile.txt

2. **Decorator Pattern**

- **What is it?**

  A pattern used to add new behavior to objects without modifying their original structure.

- **When to use?**

  When you want to add features dynamically without changing the base implementation.

- **Example:**

```go
package main

import (
    "fmt"
    "strings"
)

type Reader interface {
    Read() string
}

type FileReader struct{}
func (f FileReader) Read() string {
    return "hello world"
}

type UppercaseDecorator struct {
    Reader
}

func (u UppercaseDecorator) Read() string {
    return strings.ToUpper(u.Reader.Read())
}
```

```go
func main() {
    var r Reader = FileReader{}
    r = UppercaseDecorator{Reader: r}
    fmt.Println(r.Read())
}
```

- **Output:**

```
HELLO WORLD
```

3. **Dependency Injection**

   - **What is it?**

   A pattern where objects receive their dependencies (like services or interfaces) from outside rather than creating them internally.

   - **When to use?**

   To decouple code and make testing easier.

   - **Example:**

```go
package main

import "fmt"

type Notifier interface {
    Notify(msg string)
}

type EmailNotifier struct{}
func (e EmailNotifier) Notify(msg string) {
    fmt.Println("Email sent:", msg)
}
```

```go
type Service struct {
    Notifier Notifier
}

func (s Service) Alert(msg string) {
    s.Notifier.Notify(msg)
}

func main() {
    email := EmailNotifier{}
    service := Service{Notifier: email}
    service.Alert("Server down!")
}
```

- **Output:**

```
Email sent: Server down!
```

4. **Adapter Pattern**

   - **What is it?**

   A pattern used to make two incompatible interfaces work together.

   - **When to use?**

   When you want to integrate a component that doesn't match the existing interface.

   - **Example:**

```go
package main

import "fmt"

type Target interface {
    Request() string
}
```

```go
type Adaptee struct{}
func (a Adaptee) SpecificRequest() string {
    return "adaptee response"
}

type Adapter struct {
    Adaptee
}

func (a Adapter) Request() string {
    return a.SpecificRequest()
}

func main() {
    var t Target = Adapter{Adaptee{}}
    fmt.Println(t.Request())
}
```

- **Output:**

```
adaptee response
```

5. **Plug-In Architecture**

   - **What is it?**

   A pattern to support modular and extensible applications by loading behavior via interfaces.

   - **When to use?**

   When you need a flexible architecture to support user-defined modules.

   - **Example:**

   ```go
   package main

   import "fmt"
   ```

```go
type Plugin interface {
    Execute()
}

type HelloPlugin struct{}
func (h HelloPlugin) Execute() {
    fmt.Println("Hello from plugin!")
}

func runPlugin(p Plugin) {
    p.Execute()
}

func main() {
    plugin := HelloPlugin{}
    runPlugin(plugin)
}
```

- **Output:**

```
Hello from plugin!
```

These patterns not only demonstrate the versatility of Go interfaces but also teach you how to design reusable and clean code. Each example showcases a minimal, working implementation to help you practice and understand when and how to use them.

Programming Exercises

Easy:

1. Define an interface Notifier and implement it using Email and SMS types.

2. Write a function that takes an interface{} and prints its type using reflection.

Medium:

1. Create a program with an interface `Animal` with methods `Speak()` and `Move()`. Implement `Dog` and `Bird`.

2. Use a type switch to process a slice of `interface{}` values of different types.

Advanced:

1. Design a logging system using decorator interfaces that can log to console, file, and remote server.

2. Build a plug-in-based calculator where operations (Add, Subtract, etc.) are implemented as plug-ins using interfaces.

Summary

- Interfaces allow you to write **flexible, maintainable, and testable** Go code.

- They support polymorphism, separation of concerns, and runtime behavior injection.

- Use **empty interfaces sparingly** and avoid overusing **reflection**.

- Go interfaces are simple yet powerful tools to build robust and clean architecture.

Interview Questions: Interfaces
What?

1. What is an interface in Go, and how is it different from a struct?

2. What is the `interface{}` type, and why is it called the empty interface?

3. What are some real-world scenarios where interfaces are used effectively in Go?

Why?

1. Why is polymorphism important in Go, and how do interfaces enable it?

2. Why does Go not support explicit implementation of interfaces (like in Java or C#)?

3. Why should you avoid overusing the empty interface in Go?

How?

1. How can you use interfaces to write flexible and testable code in Go?

2. How does the Go runtime internally represent an interface?

3. How can you safely extract the underlying value of an empty interface using type assertions or type switches?

4. How would you implement a custom error type using the error interface?

Code Output

1. What will be the output of the following code snippet?

```go
package main

import "fmt"

type Speaker interface {
    Speak() string
}
```

```go
type Human struct{}

func (h Human) Speak() string {
    return "Hello, I am a human!"
}

type Robot struct{}

func (r Robot) Speak() string {
    return "Beep bop, I am a robot!"
}

func main() {
    var s Speaker
    s = Human{}
    fmt.Println(s.Speak())

    s = Robot{}
    fmt.Println(s.Speak())
}
```

2. What will be the output of the following code
    snippet, and why?

```go
package main

import "fmt"

type Animal interface {
    Speak() string
}

type Dog struct{}

func (d *Dog) Speak() string {
    return "Woof"
}
```

```
func main() {
    var a Animal
    d := Dog{}
    a = &d
    fmt.Println(a.Speak())
}
```

3. What will happen if you attempt to assign a value of a type that does not implement all methods of an interface? Provide an example.

4. What will be the output of the following code snippet?

```
package main

import "fmt"

func describe(i interface{}) {
    fmt.Printf("Value: %v, Type: %T\n", i, i)
}

func main() {
    describe(42)
    describe("Go Programming")
    describe([]int{1, 2, 3})
}
```

Practical Questions

1. Create a function that takes an interface and checks if the underlying type is a string. If yes, it should return the string in uppercase; otherwise, return "Invalid type".

GitHub Project Demonstrating Interfaces

To help you practice and understand interfaces, we have created a GitHub repository with sample programs:

- **Repository Name**: `golang-interfaces-demo`

- **Repository URL**: `https://github.com/` `rahulsidpatil/golang-interfaces-demo`

The repository contains

- Solutions to programming problems in this section

- Answers to Interview Questions along with explanation

Clone the repository and explore the examples:

```
git clone https://github.com/rahulsidpatil/golang-
interfaces-demo.git
```

4.13 Concurrency with Goroutines

Concurrency in Go is one of its most powerful features, and it's made simple with the use of `goroutines` and channels. Let's explore it from a beginner's perspective with clear examples and outputs.

4.13.1 Introduction to Goroutines

- **What is it?**

  A **goroutine** is a lightweight thread managed by the Go runtime. It allows you to run functions or methods **concurrently**, meaning they can perform tasks at the same time.

- **Why is it useful?**

  Goroutines help improve performance and responsiveness in your applications. They allow you to

  - Handle multiple requests simultaneously in web servers.

  - Perform background tasks (like logging, downloading, etc.) while continuing with the main task

  - Speed up computation by dividing work among multiple goroutines

- **Where is it used?**

  - Web servers (handling multiple requests)

  - Real-time systems (like chat apps)

  - Batch processing (running tasks in parallel)

  - Game engines, simulations, and CLI tools

- **How does the Go Compiler and runtime view it?**

  The **Go runtime** is a set of components that manage goroutines efficiently. Unlike operating system threads, goroutines

  - Use very little memory (starting with 2 KB of stack)

  - Are scheduled by Go's own scheduler

  - Are **multiplexed** on fewer OS threads, which reduces overhead

  This makes them very efficient for running thousands of concurrent tasks.

211

Example: Basic Goroutine

```go
package main

import (
    "fmt"
    "time"
)

func sayHello() {
    for i := 0; i < 3; i++ {
        fmt.Println("Hello")
        time.Sleep(100 * time.Millisecond)
    }
}

func main() {
    go sayHello() // Starts a new goroutine

    for i := 0; i < 3; i++ {
        fmt.Println("World")
        time.Sleep(100 * time.Millisecond)
    }
}
```

Sample Output (order may vary):

```
World
Hello
World
Hello
World
Hello
```

The function `sayHello()` runs in a separate goroutine, while the main function prints "World". Due to concurrent execution, the output may interleave.

Example 2: Running Multiple Goroutines

```go
package main

import (
    "fmt"
    "time"
)

func printMessage(msg string) {
    for i := 0; i < 3; i++ {
        fmt.Println(msg)
        time.Sleep(200 * time.Millisecond)
    }
}

func main() {
    go printMessage("Apple")
    go printMessage("Banana")

    time.Sleep(1 * time.Second)
    fmt.Println("Main function finished")
}
```

Sample Output:

```
Apple
Banana
Apple
Banana
```

```
Apple
Banana
Main function finished
```

We used `time.Sleep(1 * time.Second)` in `main()` to give goroutines time to complete. Without it, the main program might finish before the goroutines run.

Best Practices for Beginners

- Always assume the main function **may exit** before goroutines complete.

- Use synchronization tools like `sync.WaitGroup` (a WaitGroup is used to wait for a collection of goroutines to finish executing) or channels to **coordinate** goroutines.

- **Programming Exercises:**

   1. Write a program to print numbers from two goroutines concurrently.

   2. Implement a program to calculate the sum of elements in an array using multiple goroutines.

Channels for Communication Between Goroutines

- **What is it?**

   A **channel** in Go is a typed conduit through which goroutines can communicate. It allows one goroutine to send data and another to receive that data.

- **Why is it useful?**

  Channels eliminate the need for explicit locking by enabling communication-based concurrency. They help goroutines coordinate by passing messages, not shared memory.

- **Where is it used?**

  Common patterns include

  - **Producer-Consumer**: A goroutine produces values sent to a channel, another consumes them.

  - **Pipelining**: A series of goroutines pass data along a chain via channels.

  - **Signaling**: Channels can be used to notify or synchronize between tasks.

- **How does the Go Compiler view it?**

  Channels are first-class citizens in Go, meaning they can be passed around just like any other variable. Channels are strongly typed and can be either **buffered** (asynchronous) or **unbuffered** (synchronous).

Example 1: Basic Unbuffered Channel

```
package main

import "fmt"

func sayHello(ch chan string) {
    ch <- "Hello from goroutine!"
}
```

```
func main() {
    messageChan := make(chan string)
    go sayHello(messageChan)

    message := <-messageChan
    fmt.Println(message)
}
```

Output:

```
Hello from goroutine!
```

- In this program, a string is sent from a goroutine to
  the main function using an unbuffered channel. The
  receive operation blocks until the send completes.

Example 2: Using Channels to Sum Numbers

```
package main

import "fmt"

func sum(numbers []int, resultChan chan int) {
    sum := 0
    for _, num := range numbers {
        sum += num
    }
    resultChan <- sum
}

func main() {
    numbers := []int{1, 2, 3, 4, 5}
    resultChan := make(chan int)

    go sum(numbers, resultChan)
```

```
    result := <-resultChan
    fmt.Println("Sum:", result)
}
```

Output:

```
Sum: 15
```

- The sum of numbers is computed in a separate goroutine and passed back to the main function through a channel.

Example 3: Buffered Channel

```
package main
import "fmt"
func main() {
    ch := make(chan int, 2) // Buffered channel with
                                        capacity 2
    ch <- 1
    ch <- 2
    fmt.Println(<-ch)
    fmt.Println(<-ch)
}
```

Output:

```
1
2
```

- Buffered channels allow sending without blocking until the buffer is full.

Example 4: Channel-Based Pipeline

```go
package main

import "fmt"

func generate(nums ...int) <-chan int {
    out := make(chan int)
    go func() {
        for _, n := range nums {
            out <- n
        }
        close(out)
    }()
    return out
}

func square(in <-chan int) <-chan int {
    out := make(chan int)
    go func() {
        for n := range in {
            out <- n * n
        }
        close(out)
    }()
    return out
}

func main() {
    numbers := generate(2, 3, 4)
    squared := square(numbers)
```

```
    for result := range squared {
        fmt.Println(result)
    }
}
```

Output:

```
4
9
16
```

- This demonstrates a pipeline where one goroutine generates numbers and another squares them. Channels are used to pass data between stages.

Example 5: Using Channels for Signaling

```
package main

import (
    "fmt"
    "time"
)

func task(done chan bool) {
    fmt.Println("Working...")
    time.Sleep(time.Second)
    fmt.Println("Done")
    done <- true
}

func main() {
    done := make(chan bool)
    go task(done)

    <-done // Wait for task to finish
}
```

Output:

```
Working...
Done
```

- A channel is used here to signal the completion of a task from a goroutine to the main function.

Channels are essential to building concurrent programs in Go. They form the foundation of many design patterns and communication strategies that make Go a great language for writing performant and scalable systems.

- **Programming Exercises:**

    1. Create a program where multiple goroutines calculate partial sums, and the main function collects and combines the results using a channel.

    2. Implement a producer-consumer model using channels.

Select Statement and Channel Operations

- **What is it?**

    The select statement in Go lets a goroutine wait on multiple communication operations (like sending or receiving on channels). Think of it as a switch for channels—it selects the first channel that is ready.

- **Why is it useful?**

  It helps you

  - Listen to multiple channels at once

  - Avoid blocking when waiting for a single channel

  - Handle timeouts and cancellations elegantly

- **Where is it used?**

  - Merging outputs from multiple goroutines

  - Implementing timeouts or default fallbacks

  - Multiplexing data from various sources

- **How does the Go Compiler handle it?**

  Go internally monitors all cases in a `select` statement. As soon as one of them is ready, it executes that case. If multiple cases are ready at the same time, one is chosen **randomly** to ensure fairness and avoid starvation.

  Example 1: Receiving from Two Channels

```
package main

import (
    "fmt"
    "time"
)

func main() {
    ch1 := make(chan string)
    ch2 := make(chan string)
```

```go
    // Simulate sending message to ch1 after 1 second
    go func() {
        time.Sleep(1 * time.Second)
        ch1 <- "Hello from Channel 1"
    }()
    // Simulate sending message to ch2 after 2 seconds
    go func() {
        time.Sleep(2 * time.Second)
        ch2 <- "Hello from Channel 2"
    }()

    for i := 0; i < 2; i++ {
        select {
        case msg1 := <-ch1:
            fmt.Println("Received:", msg1)
        case msg2 := <-ch2:
            fmt.Println("Received:", msg2)
        }
    }
}
```

Expected Output:

Received: Hello from Channel 1

Received: Hello from Channel 2

Example 2: Adding a Timeout

```go
package main
import (
    "fmt"
    "time"
)
```

```go
func main() {
    ch := make(chan string)

    select {
    case msg := <-ch:
        fmt.Println("Received:", msg)
    case <-time.After(2 * time.Second):
        fmt.Println("Timeout: no message received
        within 2 seconds")
    }
}
```

Expected Output (since no value is sent):

```
Timeout: no message received within 2 seconds
```

Example 3: Non-blocking Communication with default Case

```go
package main

import "fmt"

func main() {
    ch := make(chan int)

    select {
    case val := <-ch:
        fmt.Println("Received:", val)
    default:
        fmt.Println("No value received, moving on")
    }
}
```

Expected Output:

```
No value received, moving on
```

This example prevents the program from blocking indefinitely.

🧠 Key Takeaways

- Use `select` when you want to listen to multiple channels concurrently.

- Use `time.After` in a `select` for timeouts.

- Use `default` to perform non-blocking checks.

- Select chooses one **ready** case randomly if multiple channels are ready.

- **Programming Exercises:**

    1. Write a program to implement a timeout mechanism using the `select` statement.

    2. Create a program to merge results from multiple channels using the `select` statement.

4.13.2 Synchronization of Goroutines with Mutex and WaitGroups

When multiple goroutines access shared memory, synchronization is essential to prevent race conditions and ensure correct program behavior.

🔐 What is mutex?

A **mutex** (mutual exclusion) is a lock mechanism used to synchronize access to shared resources.

- **Use Case:** Prevent multiple goroutines from writing to the same variable at the same time.

```go
package main

import (
    "fmt"
    "sync"
)

func main() {
    var mu sync.Mutex
    counter := 0

    var wg sync.WaitGroup
    for i := 0; i < 5; i++ {
        wg.Add(1)
        go func() {
            defer wg.Done()
            mu.Lock()
            counter++
            mu.Unlock()
        }()
    }

    wg.Wait()
    fmt.Println("Final Counter:", counter)
}
```

Expected Output:

```
Final Counter: 5
```

Without the mu.Lock() and mu.Unlock(), this might result in a race condition.

⧗ What is WaitGroup?

A **WaitGroup** is used to wait for a collection of goroutines to finish executing.

- **Use Case:** Block until all spawned goroutines complete.

```
package main

import (
    "fmt"
    "sync"
)

func worker(id int, wg *sync.WaitGroup) {
    defer wg.Done()
    fmt.Println("Worker", id, "done")
}

func main() {
    var wg sync.WaitGroup
    for i := 1; i <= 3; i++ {
        wg.Add(1)
        go worker(i, &wg)
    }

    wg.Wait()
    fmt.Println("All workers completed")
}
```

Expected Output:

```
Worker 1 done
Worker 2 done
Worker 3 done
All workers completed
```

🧠 Key Concepts

- **Mutex** ensures only one goroutine accesses a block of code at a time.

- **WaitGroup** waits for multiple goroutines to finish.

- Always call Add() before launching the goroutine.

- Always call Done() in the goroutine (use defer).

🔧 Programming Exercises

1. Use a mutex to safely update a shared map across ten goroutines.

2. Launch five goroutines, each printing a message after one second. Use WaitGroup to wait for all of them to complete.

3. Combine WaitGroup and mutex to count how many times each word appears in a list of strings processed in parallel.

4. Implement a simple counter struct with increment and value methods using mutex.

These synchronization tools are fundamental for writing safe and concurrent Go programs.

Interview Questions: Concurrency with Goroutines
What?

1. What is a goroutine in Go, and how does it differ from a traditional thread?

2. What are channels in Go, and how do they facilitate communication between goroutines?

3. What is the purpose of the `select` statement in Go?

Why?

1. Why are `goroutines` considered lightweight compared to OS threads?

2. Why are channels preferred over shared memory for communication between `goroutines`?

3. Why would you use a `select` statement instead of polling multiple channels?

How?

1. How does Go's runtime manage `goroutines` efficiently?

2. How can you synchronize multiple `goroutines` without using explicit locks?

3. How can you use the `select` statement to handle a timeout in a program?

Code Output Questions

1. What will be the output of the following code snippet?

```
package main

import (
    "fmt"
    "time"
)

func main() {
    ch := make(chan int)
```

```go
go func() {
    for i := 0; i < 3; i++ {
        ch <- i
        time.Sleep(500 * time.Millisecond)
    }
    close(ch)
}()

for val := range ch {
    fmt.Println(val)
}
}
```

2. What will happen if you attempt to send data to a closed channel in Go?

3. What will be the output of the following code snippet?

```go
package main

import "fmt"

func main() {
    ch := make(chan int, 2)

    ch <- 1
    ch <- 2

    select {
    case val := <-ch:
        fmt.Println("Received:", val)
    default:
        fmt.Println("No data to receive")
    }
}
```

Problem-Solving

4. How would you implement a worker pool pattern using goroutines and channels in Go?

5. How would you design a system where goroutines communicate with each other without any deadlocks?

6. How can you use buffered channels to control the concurrency level in your program?

GitHub Project Demonstrating Concurrency with Goroutines

To help you practice and visualize concurrency in Go, we have created a GitHub repository with sample programs:

- **Repository Name**: golang-concurrency-demo

- **Repository URL**: https://github.com/ rahulsidpatil/golang-concurrency-demo

The repository contains

- Solutions to programming problems in this section

- Answers to Interview Questions along with explanation

Clone the repository and explore the examples:

```
git clone https://github.com/rahulsidpatil/golang-
concurrency-demo.git
```

4.14 Error Handling

4.14.1 Error Types in Go

- **What are they?**

  Errors in Go represent conditions where the program cannot proceed as expected.

- **Why are they useful?**

  Error handling ensures that your program can recover from unexpected states or gracefully terminate when necessary.

- **Where are they used?**

  They are found in functions and methods where something might fail, such as file operations, network communication, or user input validation.

- **How does the Go Compiler view them?**

  Errors in Go are implemented as values of the error type, which is an interface with a single method:

```go
type error interface {
    Error() string
}
```

  The compiler enforces explicit error handling, meaning errors cannot be ignored without intent. This makes Go programs more robust and predictable.

Example:

```go
package main

import (
    "errors"
    "fmt"
)

func divide(a, b int) (int, error) {
    if b == 0 {
        return 0, errors.New("division by zero")
    }
    return a / b, nil
}

func main() {
    result, err := divide(10, 0)
    if err != nil {
        fmt.Println("Error:", err)
        return
    }
    fmt.Println("Result:", result)
}
```

This program defines a divide function to perform integer division with error handling for division by zero, and in the main function, it attempts to divide ten by zero, printing an error message if division by zero occurs.

- **Programming Exercises:**

  1. Write a function to calculate the square root of a number and return an error if the input is negative.

  2. Create a program to open a file and return a custom error if the file does not exist.

4.14.2 Handling Errors Gracefully

- **What is it?**

  Graceful error handling involves checking and responding to errors in a way that does not crash the program unnecessarily.

- **Why is it useful?**

  It improves user experience and ensures stability in production environments.

- **Where is it used?**

  Common in network services, file I/O operations, and user-facing applications.

- **How does the Go Compiler view it?**

  The compiler enforces a pattern of error handling where errors must be checked explicitly. This design promotes clarity and forces developers to address potential issues.

Example:

```go
package main

import (
    "fmt"
    "os"
)

func main() {
    file, err := os.Open("nonexistent.txt")
    if err != nil {
        fmt.Println("Error opening file:", err)
        return
    }
    defer file.Close()
    fmt.Println("File opened successfully")
}
```

This program attempts to open a file named nonexistent.txt and prints an error message if the file does not exist or cannot be opened; otherwise, it prints a success message and ensures the file is properly closed before exiting.

- **Programming Exercises:**

  1. Write a program to read a file line by line and handle errors if the file cannot be read.

  2. Implement a retry mechanism for a function that may fail intermittently.

4.14.3 Creating Custom Errors

- **What are they?**

  Custom errors provide more context and detail about what went wrong in a program.

- **Why are they useful?**

  They enable better debugging and can provide meaningful feedback to users.

- **Where are they used?**

  They are common in APIs and libraries to describe specific issues encountered during execution.

- **How does the Go Compiler view them?**

  Custom errors are implemented by defining types that satisfy the error interface. This allows developers to include additional fields for context.

Example:

```go
package main

import "fmt"

type DivideError struct {
    Dividend int
    Divisor  int
}

func (e *DivideError) Error() string {
    return fmt.Sprintf("cannot divide %d by %d",
    e.Dividend, e.Divisor)
}
```

```go
func divide(a, b int) (int, error) {
    if b == 0 {
        return 0, &DivideError{Dividend: a, Divisor: b}
    }
    return a / b, nil
}

func main() {
    result, err := divide(10, 0)
    if err != nil {
        fmt.Println("Error:", err)
        return
    }
    fmt.Println("Result:", result)
}
```

This program attempts to divide two integers, and if the divisor is zero, it returns a custom error indicating the division is not possible; otherwise, it computes and prints the result of the division.

- **Programming Exercises:**

    1. Create a custom error type for validating user input (e.g., age must be greater than 0).

    2. Write a program to simulate a banking system where custom errors are used for insufficient funds.

Interview Questions: Error Handling

1. What is the error type in Go, and why is it important?

2. Why does Go enforce explicit error handling?

3. How can you create a custom error in Go?

4. What is the output of the following code snippet?

```go
package main

import "fmt"

func main() {
    err := fmt.Errorf("an error occurred: %d", 404)
    if err != nil {
        fmt.Println(err)
    }
}
```

5. Why would you use a defer statement in error handling?

6. What are the advantages of using custom error types?

7. How do you handle errors in a REST API written in Go?

8. What will be the output of this code snippet?

```go
package main

import "errors"

func main() {
    err := errors.New("error example")
    fmt.Println(err)
}
```

9. What is a common pattern for retrying operations after a transient error in Go?

10. How does the errors.Is function work, and when would you use it?

11. Why is it better to return an error instead of panicking in most situations?

12. What will be the output of the following code?

```go
package main

import "fmt"

type MyError struct {}

func (e MyError) Error() string {
    return "This is my custom error"
}

func main() {
    err := MyError{}
    fmt.Println(err)
}
```

13. What are the key differences between errors.New and fmt.Errorf?

14. How would you implement error wrapping in Go, and what are its benefits?

15. What steps would you take to log errors effectively in a distributed system?

GitHub Project Demonstrating Error Handling

To help you practice and visualize error handling, we have created a GitHub repository with sample programs:

- **Repository Name**: golang-error-handling-demo

- **Repository URL**: https://github.com/ rahulsidpatil/golang-error-handling-demo

The repository contains

- Solutions to programming problems in this section

- Answers to Interview Questions along with explanation

Clone the repository and explore the examples:

```
git clone https://github.com/rahulsidpatil/golang-error-
handling-demo.git
```

4.15 File I/O

File I/O (Input/Output) is an essential feature in any programming language, enabling applications to persist data, process input from files, and generate output files. Go provides a rich set of utilities in the os and io packages to handle file operations efficiently.

4.15.1 Reading from and Writing to Files

What is it?

Reading and writing files involves accessing the file system to retrieve or store data in a file.

Why is it useful?

It enables applications to manage persistent storage, interact with external data sources, and generate outputs.

Where is it used?

It is used in applications requiring configuration files, data processing, logs, and report generation.

How does the Go Compiler view it?

The Go runtime treats files as streams of bytes. The os package provides functions like Open, Create, and Read for direct interaction with files. The compiler ensures efficient buffering and system call handling.

Example:

```go
package main

import (
    "fmt"
    "os"
)

func main() {
    // Writing to a file
    file, err := os.Create("example.txt")
    if err != nil {
        fmt.Println("Error creating file:", err)
        return
    }
    defer file.Close()

    file.WriteString("Hello, File I/O in Go!")
    fmt.Println("Data written to file")

    // Reading from a file
    file, err = os.Open("example.txt")
    if err != nil {
        fmt.Println("Error opening file:", err)
        return
    }
```

```
    defer file.Close()

    buffer := make([]byte, 100)
    n, _ := file.Read(buffer)
    fmt.Println("File content:", string(buffer[:n]))
}
```

This program demonstrates basic file I/O operations by creating a file named example.txt, writing a string to it, reading the content back, and printing the content to the console.

Programming Exercises:

1. Write a program to count the number of lines in a text file.

2. Create a function to append data to an existing file.

4.15.2 Working with Buffers

What are they?

Buffers provide a way to read and write data in chunks, improving performance and reducing memory usage.

Why are they useful?

They are useful for handling large files or streams where reading/writing all at once is impractical.

Where are they used?

They are found in applications processing large datasets, network streams, or log files.

How does the Go Compiler view them?

The bufio package wraps file operations with buffered readers and writers. This minimizes system calls by batching reads and writes, leading to better performance.

Example:

```go
package main

import (
    "bufio"
    "fmt"
    "os"
)

func main() {
    file, err := os.Open("example.txt")
    if err != nil {
        fmt.Println("Error opening file:", err)
        return
    }
    defer file.Close()

    reader := bufio.NewReader(file)
    line, _ := reader.ReadString('\n')
    fmt.Println("Read line:", line)
}
```

This Go program opens a file named example.txt, reads the first line from it, and prints that line to the console.

Programming Exercises:

1. Write a program to read a file line by line and print each line.

2. Implement a buffered writer to write multiple lines into a file efficiently.

4.15.3 Error Checking in File Operations

What is it?

Error checking ensures that file operations are executed correctly and handles failures gracefully.

Why is it useful?

It prevents unexpected crashes and helps debug issues related to file access.

Where is it used?

It is used in all applications interacting with the file system, especially when user-provided paths or external files are involved.

How does the Go Compiler view it?

Go requires explicit error handling. Functions interacting with files return an error type, which must be checked to prevent runtime issues.

Example:

```go
package main

import (
    "fmt"
    "os"
)

func main() {
    _, err := os.Open("nonexistent.txt")
    if err != nil {
        fmt.Println("Error occurred:", err)
    } else {
        fmt.Println("File opened successfully")
    }
}
```

This program attempts to open a file named nonexistent.txt, and if the file does not exist or an error occurs, it prints an error message; otherwise, it prints a success message.

Programming Exercises:

1. Write a program to safely delete a file if it exists.

2. Create a function to check if a file is readable and writable.

Interview Questions: File I/O

1. **What?**

   - What is file I/O in Go?

   - What are the primary packages used for file operations in Go?

   - What is the role of the bufio package in Go?

2. **Why?**

   - Why is error handling crucial in file operations?

   - Why is buffered I/O preferred for large files or streams?

   - Why do file operations in Go require explicit handling of the error type?

3. **How?**

   - How does Go handle file creation and opening?

   - How can you read a file line by line using Go?

   - How do you append data to an existing file in Go?

4. **What will be the output of this code snippet?**

- **Code Snippet 1:**

```
package main

import (
    "fmt"
    "os"
)

func main() {
    file, err := os.Create("output.txt")
    if err != nil {
        fmt.Println("Error:", err)
        return
    }
    defer file.Close()

    file.WriteString("Go Programming")
    fmt.Println("File written")
}
```

What will happen if the file output.txt
already exists?

- **Code Snippet 2:**

```
package main

import (
    "bufio"
    "fmt"
    "os"
)
```

245

```go
func main() {
    file, err := os.Open("example.txt")
    if err != nil {
        fmt.Println("Error:", err)
        return
    }
    defer file.Close()

    scanner := bufio.NewScanner(file)
    for scanner.Scan() {
        fmt.Println(scanner.Text())
    }
}
```

What will the program output if the file example.txt is empty?

5. **What?**

   - What is the difference between os.Open and os.Create in Go?

   - What is a buffered writer, and how does it improve file writing performance?

6. **Why?**

   - Why does Go use defer for file operations?

   - Why is it essential to check for EOF when reading files?

7. **How?**

   - How do you ensure that file handles are properly closed after use in Go?

   - How can you safely check if a file exists before attempting to read it?

8. **What will be the output of this code snippet?**

   - **Code Snippet 3:**

   ```go
   package main

   import (
       "fmt"
       "os"
   )

   func main() {
       file, err := os.Open("nonexistent.txt")
       if err != nil {
           fmt.Println("Error opening file:", err)
           return
       }
       defer file.Close()
       fmt.Println("File opened successfully")
   }
   ```

   What will the output be if the file nonexistent.
   txt does not exist?

   - **Code Snippet 4:**

   ```go
   package main

   import (
       "fmt"
       "os"
   )

   func main() {
       file, err := os.Create("test.txt")
   ```

```go
    if err != nil {
        fmt.Println("Error:", err)
        return
    }
    defer file.Close()

    _, err = file.WriteString("Hello")
    if err != nil {
        fmt.Println("Write error:", err)
    }

    _, err = os.Stat("test.txt")
    if err != nil {
        fmt.Println("Stat error:", err)
    } else {
        fmt.Println("File exists")
    }
}
```

What will the program print if the file creation fails?

GitHub Project Demonstrating File I/O

To practice these file I/O concepts, we have created a GitHub repository:

- **Repository Name**: golang-file-io-demo

- **Repository URL**: https://github.com/ rahulsidpatil/golang-file-io-demo

The repository contains

- Solutions to programming problems in this section

- Answers to Interview Questions along with explanation

Clone the repository and explore the examples:

```
git clone https://github.com/rahulsidpatil/golang-file-
io-demo.git
```

4.16 Unit Testing

Unit testing is an essential practice in software development that ensures individual units of your code work as expected. Go's standard library provides robust support for testing and benchmarking, allowing developers to write, run, and measure tests efficiently.

4.16.1 Testing and Benchmarking

What is unit testing?

Unit testing involves testing individual functions or methods to ensure they perform as intended. It helps catch bugs early in the development cycle.

Why is it useful?

Unit testing provides confidence that your code behaves as expected, simplifies debugging, and facilitates changes by ensuring that existing functionality is not broken.

Where is it used?

It is used in all stages of software development, especially when implementing critical features, refactoring code, or developing libraries and APIs.

How does the Go Compiler view it?

The Go toolchain includes a `testing` package that supports writing unit tests and benchmarks. Test files are named with the `_test.go` suffix and include functions following the `TestXxx` pattern. These test functions accept a pointer to `testing.T`, which provides methods for reporting test failures and logs.

- **Example: Writing Unit Tests**

```
package mathutil

import "testing"

func Add(a, b int) int {
    return a + b
}

func TestAdd(t *testing.T) {
    result := Add(2, 3)
    expected := 5
    if result != expected {
        t.Errorf("Add(2, 3) = %d; want %d", result,
        expected)
    }
}
```

This example defines a simple Add function and its corresponding unit test. Running go test executes the test and reports any failures.

- **Example: Writing Benchmarks**

Go also supports benchmarking to measure code performance. Benchmark functions follow the BenchmarkXxx naming pattern and use a pointer to testing.B:

```
func BenchmarkAdd(b *testing.B) {
    for i := 0; i < b.N; i++ {
        Add(2, 3)
    }
}
```

Running go `test -bench .` executes the benchmark and provides performance metrics.

- **Programming Exercises:**

    1. Write a unit test for a function that calculates the factorial of a number.

    2. Benchmark a function that sorts an array of integers.

Interview Questions: Unit Testing
What?

1. What is the purpose of unit testing in Go?

2. What naming conventions should be followed for test files and test functions in Go?

3. What is the `testing` package used for in Go?

Why?

1. Why is it important to test individual units of code?

2. Why does the `testing.T` parameter play a crucial role in test functions?

3. Why is benchmarking important in the context of performance testing?

How?

1. How do you write a test function in Go? Explain with an example.

2. How can you use `t.Errorf` to handle test failures gracefully?

3. How do you run benchmarks in Go, and what command is used?

Code Output Questions

1. What will be the output of the following code
    snippet?

```go
func Multiply(a, b int) int {
    return a * b
}

func TestMultiply(t *testing.T) {
    result := Multiply(2, 0)
    expected := 0
    if result != expected {
        t.Errorf("Multiply(2, 0) = %d; want %d",
        result, expected)
    }
}
```

2. What will be the output of running the benchmark
    function for the Add function provided earlier?

3. What happens if the t.Fail() method is used in a
    test function?

Practical Questions

4. How do you handle dependencies or mock external
    calls in unit testing?

5. How can you measure test coverage in a Go project?

6. How do you structure test cases for edge
    conditions in Go?

GitHub Project Demonstrating Unit Testing Concepts

To help you practice and explore testing and benchmarking in Go, we have
created a GitHub repository:

- **Repository Name**: golang-testing-demo

- **Repository URL**: https://github.com/
  rahulsidpatil/golang-testing-demo

The repository contains

- Solutions to programming problems in this section

- Answers to Interview Questions along with explanation

Clone the repository and explore the examples:

```
git clone https://github.com/rahulsidpatil/golang-
testing-demo.git
cd golang-testing-demo
```

4.17 Useful Go Programming Constructs

4.17.1 Timers and Tickers

What are they?
Timers and tickers are constructs in the time package that help manage
tasks scheduled to run at specific intervals or after a delay.

Why are they useful?
They allow efficient scheduling of time-based operations, such as periodic
updates, reminders, or delays in execution.

Where are they used?
Commonly used in applications like real-time monitoring, polling, and
retry mechanisms.

How does the Go Compiler view them?

The compiler treats timers and tickers as resources that allocate and manage their state within the runtime's scheduler. It ensures minimal resource usage by leveraging Go's efficient goroutine model to implement time-based callbacks.

Example:

```go
package main

import (
    "fmt"
    "time"
)

func main() {
    // Timer example
    timer := time.NewTimer(2 * time.Second)
    fmt.Println("Timer started")
    <-timer.C
    fmt.Println("Timer expired")

    // Ticker example
    ticker := time.NewTicker(1 * time.Second)
    done := make(chan bool)

    go func() {
        time.Sleep(5 * time.Second)
        done <- true
    }()

    for {
        select {
        case <-done:
            ticker.Stop()
```

```
        fmt.Println("Ticker stopped")
        return
    case t := <-ticker.C:
        fmt.Println("Tick at", t)
    }
  }
}
```

This program demonstrates the usage of a time.Timer to execute a task after a delay and a time.Ticker to perform a recurring task at regular intervals until stopped.

Programming Exercises:

1. Write a program that prints the current time every second for ten seconds using a ticker.

2. Create a countdown timer that counts down from ten seconds and prints "Time's up!" when complete.

4.17.2 Worker Pools

What are they?
A worker pool is a pattern used to manage a fixed number of goroutines that execute tasks concurrently.

Why are they useful?
They optimize resource usage by controlling the number of goroutines and managing task execution efficiently.

Where are they used?
They are ideal for scenarios like processing jobs from a queue, performing concurrent HTTP requests, or parallel computation.

How does the Go Compiler view them?

Worker pools leverage Go's goroutines and channels for communication. The compiler optimizes these constructs for lightweight concurrency and efficient scheduling.

Example:

```go
package main

import (
    "fmt"
    "sync"
)

func worker(id int, jobs <-chan int, results chan<- int, wg
*sync.WaitGroup) {
    defer wg.Done()
    for job := range jobs {
        fmt.Printf("Worker %d processing job %d\n", id, job)
        results <- job * 2
    }
}

func main() {
    const numJobs = 5
    const numWorkers = 3

    jobs := make(chan int, numJobs)
    results := make(chan int, numJobs)

    var wg sync.WaitGroup

    for w := 1; w <= numWorkers; w++ {
        wg.Add(1)
        go worker(w, jobs, results, &wg)
    }
```

```go
    for j := 1; j <= numJobs; j++ {
        jobs <- j
    }
    close(jobs)

    wg.Wait()
    close(results)

    for result := range results {
        fmt.Println("Result:", result)
    }
}
```

This program demonstrates a worker pool pattern where multiple workers (goroutines) process jobs from a channel concurrently, perform a calculation (doubling the job value), and send the results to another channel, with synchronization managed using a sync.WaitGroup.

Programming Exercises:

1. Implement a worker pool to calculate the squares of numbers from one to ten.

2. Write a program that uses a worker pool to fetch and print the content of multiple URLs concurrently.

4.17.3 Contexts

What are they?

Contexts provide a way to manage deadlines, cancellations, and other request-scoped values across API boundaries.

Why are they useful?

They enable graceful termination of processes, avoiding resource leaks in concurrent programs.

Where are they used?

They are commonly used in server applications, database queries, and long-running tasks.

How does the Go Compiler view them?

Contexts are implemented as immutable structs with methods to derive child contexts. The compiler and runtime work together to propagate deadlines and cancellations efficiently.

Example:

```go
package main

import (
    "context"
    "fmt"
    "time"
)

func main() {
    ctx, cancel := context.WithTimeout(context.Background(),
    2*time.Second)
    defer cancel()

    done := make(chan bool)
    go func() {
        time.Sleep(3 * time.Second)
        done <- true
    }()

    select {
    case <-ctx.Done():
        fmt.Println("Context timed out:", ctx.Err())
    case <-done:
        fmt.Println("Task completed")
    }
}
```

This program demonstrates the use of a context.WithTimeout to enforce a two-second timeout for a task running in a separate goroutine, which sleeps for three seconds, ultimately causing the context to time out before the task completes, resulting in the message "Context timed out: context deadline exceeded" being printed.

Programming Exercises:

1. Write a program using context to cancel a goroutine after five seconds.

2. Create a function that fetches data from a URL with a context deadline.

4.17.4 Circuit Breakers

What are they?

Circuit breakers are patterns that protect systems from cascading failures by breaking the circuit when errors exceed a threshold.

Why are they useful?

They enhance system reliability by preventing repeated failures from overwhelming services.

Where are they used?

They are commonly implemented in microservices, networked applications, and APIs.

How does the Go Compiler view them?

Circuit breakers are implemented at the application level. The compiler ensures efficient execution of their logic, leveraging goroutines and channels where necessary.

Example:

```go
package main

import (
    "fmt"
    "math/rand"
    "sync"
    "time"
)

type CircuitBreaker struct {
    failures    int
    threshold   int
    resetTime   time.Duration
    state       string
    mutex       sync.Mutex
}

func NewCircuitBreaker(threshold int, resetTime time.Duration)
*CircuitBreaker {
    return &CircuitBreaker{threshold: threshold, resetTime:
    resetTime, state: "closed"}
}

func (cb *CircuitBreaker) Call(task func() error) error {
    cb.mutex.Lock()
    if cb.state == "open" {
        cb.mutex.Unlock()
        return fmt.Errorf("circuit breaker is open")
    }
    cb.mutex.Unlock()
```

```
    err := task()
    cb.mutex.Lock()
    defer cb.mutex.Unlock()
    if err != nil {
        cb.failures++
        if cb.failures >= cb.threshold {
            cb.state = "open"
            go cb.reset()
        }
    } else {
        cb.failures = 0
    }
    return err
}

func (cb *CircuitBreaker) reset() {
    time.Sleep(cb.resetTime)
    cb.mutex.Lock()
    cb.state = "closed"
    cb.failures = 0
    cb.mutex.Unlock()
}

func main() {
    cb := NewCircuitBreaker(3, 5*time.Second)
    task := func() error {
        if rand.Intn(2) == 0 {
            return fmt.Errorf("task failed")
        }
        return nil
    }
```

```
for i := 0; i < 10; i++ {
    err := cb.Call(task)
    if err != nil {
        fmt.Println("Attempt", i+1, "failed:", err)
    } else {
        fmt.Println("Attempt", i+1, "succeeded")
    }
    time.Sleep(1 * time.Second)
}
}
```

This program implements a circuit breaker pattern to manage task execution, where it tracks failures of a task function and temporarily blocks further execution ("opens the circuit") if failures exceed a threshold, resetting the state ("closing the circuit") after a specified reset time.

Programming Exercises:

1. Implement a circuit breaker to protect a database connection.

2. Write a program to simulate a circuit breaker for an HTTP API.

To help you practice and explore testing and benchmarking in Go, we have created a GitHub repository:

- **Repository Name**: useful-go-constructs

- **Repository URL**: https://github.com/ rahulsidpatil/useful-go-constructs

The repository contains

- Solutions to programming problems in this section

- Answers to Interview Questions along with explanation

Clone the repository and explore the examples:

```
git clone https://github.com/rahulsidpatil/useful-go-
constructs.git
cd useful-go-constructs
```

4.18 Summary

This chapter provided a comprehensive overview of the core concepts of the Go programming language, focusing on its simplicity, efficiency, and scalability. By understanding Go's unique approach to data types, operators, control flow, functions, and methods, readers are now equipped to create robust and idiomatic applications. Key topics included

1. **Go's Primitive and Composite Data Types**: Exploring `int`, `float`, `bool`, `string`, `rune`, arrays, slices, maps, and structs

2. **Operators and Expressions**: Learning arithmetic, comparison, and logical operators to build effective computational logic

3. **Control Flow**: Understanding conditional statements (`if`, `else`, `switch`), loops, and defer/panic/recover mechanisms

4. **Functions**: Building reusable and modular code with parameters, return values, closures, and variadic functions

5. **Pointers**: Leveraging memory addresses for efficient data manipulation and in-place updates

6. **Structs and Methods**: Modeling real-world entities and associating behaviors through methods

7. **Interfaces**: Embracing polymorphism for flexible and reusable designs

8. **Concurrency with Goroutines**: Harnessing lightweight threads and channels for parallelism

9. **Error Handling**: Managing program errors gracefully to enhance reliability

4.18.1 What's Next?

In the next chapter, we will dive into a hands-on project to apply the foundational knowledge gained in this chapter. Readers will learn how to design, implement, and deploy a command-line interface (CLI) tool using Go, incorporating best practices and essential development tools.

CHAPTER 5

Building and Deploying a Useful CLI Tool

5.1 Introduction

In the previous chapter, we explored core Go programming concepts. Now, we turn theory into practice by building and releasing a **real-world open source CLI tool**. You will not only write a fully functional command-line application but also learn how to organize your project, automate tasks with a Makefile, and distribute it via GitHub.

By the end of this chapter, you will

1. Understand what CLI tools are and where they're used

2. Learn how to develop and structure a CLI tool in Go

3. Use Git and GitHub for source control and collaboration

© Rahul Sid Patil 2025
R. S. Patil, *Let Us Go!*, https://doi.org/10.1007/979-8-8688-1442-6_5

4. Automate project tasks using a Makefile

5. Publish your CLI tool as an open source project

We'll build a simple **password generator CLI tool** in Go and deploy it as a public GitHub project. Let's dive in.

5.2 What Is a CLI Tool?

A **command-line interface (CLI) tool** is a program run from the terminal, accepting commands or flags and returning output to the console.

5.2.1 ✎ Common Use Cases

- **Automation**: File operations, scripts, backups
- **Data Processing**: Parsing, filtering, formatting
- **DevOps**: Deployment, builds, config management
- **Development Tools**: Compilers, linters, formatters

5.2.2 ◉ Popular CLI Tools Written in Go

- docker: Container management
- kubectl: Kubernetes command-line interface
- hugo: Static site generator
- terraform: Infrastructure as code

5.3 Introduction to Open Source Software

Open source software allows anyone to read, modify, and distribute the source code. It promotes transparency, learning, and global collaboration.

5.3.1 ☑ Benefits

- Encourages contributions from developers worldwide

- Builds a strong portfolio

- Improves understanding of project structures, testing, and best practices

5.3.2 ✍ Best Practices

1. **License**: Use MIT, Apache 2.0, or GPL.

2. **Documentation**: Create a detailed README.md.

3. **Community**: Encourage issues and contributions.

4. **Version Control**: Use Git/GitHub for collaborative development.

5.4 Step by Step: Build and Release a CLI Password Generator in Go

5.4.1 ☺ Problem Statement

Build a cross-platform password generator as a CLI tool in Go and release it as an open source project.

5.4.2 Create GitHub Repository

1. Visit https://github.com.

2. Create a new repository named password-generator.

3. Clone it locally:

```
git clone https://github.com/<your-username>
/password-generator.git
cd password-generator
```

� **Replace** <your-username> **with your actual GitHub username.**

For example:

```
git clone https://github.com/rahulsidpatil/
password-generator.git
cd password-generator
```

5.4.3 Set Up Go Module

```
go mod init github.com/rahulsidpatil/password-generator
```

5.4.4 Write the Go Code

Create a file named main.go:

```
package main

import (
```

```go
    "crypto/rand"
    "flag"
    "fmt"
    "math/big"
)

func main() {
    length := flag.Int("length", 12, "Length of the password")
    includeSpecial := flag.Bool("special", false, "Include
    special characters")
    flag.Parse()

    password := generatePassword(*length, *includeSpecial)
    fmt.Printf("Generated Password: %s\n", password)
}

func generatePassword(length int, special bool) string {
    letters := "abcdefghijklmnopqrstuvwxyzABCDEFGHIJKLMNOPQRST
    UVWXYZ0123456789"
    if special {
        letters += "!@#$%^&*()-_=+"
    }

    password := make([]byte, length)
    for i := range password {
        randIndex, _ := rand.Int(rand.Reader, big.NewInt(int64
        (len(letters))))
        password[i] = letters[randIndex.Int64()]
    }
    return string(password)
}
```

☑ **Sample Output**:

```
$ go run main.go --length=16 --special
Generated Password: aG#3sF$9mN1qZ&7W
```

▨ **Go flag package**

▨ **Go crypto/rand package**

❶ **Note**   This code is for educational purposes and uses a common password generation pattern found in Go learning resources.

5.4.5 Add a Makefile

Create a file named Makefile:

```
BINARY_NAME=password-generator

build:
        go build -o $(BINARY_NAME)

clean:
        rm -f $(BINARY_NAME) $(BINARY_NAME).exe || true

test:
        go test ./...

run:
        ./$(BINARY_NAME) --length=12 --special

release:
        GOOS=windows GOARCH=amd64 go build -o $(BINARY_NAME).exe
        GOOS=linux GOARCH=amd64 go build -o $(BINARY_NAME)
        GOOS=darwin GOARCH=amd64 go build -o $(BINARY_NAME)
```

☑ **Usage**:

```
make build
make run
make release
```

5.4.6 Add Unit Tests (Optional but Recommended)

Create a test file password_test.go:

```
package main

import "testing"

func TestGeneratePassword(t *testing.T) {
    pass := generatePassword(10, true)
    if len(pass) != 10 {
        t.Errorf("Expected length 10, got %d", len(pass))
    }
}
```

Run tests:

```
make test
```

5.4.7 Add License and README

License

Use a license such as MIT License.

README.md

```
# Password Generator CLI Tool

## Prerequisites
```

```
- Go 1.21 or later

## Installation
```bash
git clone https://github.com/rahulsidpatil/password-
generator.git
cd password-generator
make build
```

Usage

```
./password-generator --length=16 --special
```

Contributing

1. Fork the repo.

2. Create a branch: `git checkout -b feature-name`.

3. Commit and push.

4. Submit a pull request.

```
---
```

5.4.8 Commit and Push to GitHub

```bash
git add .
git commit -m "Initial commit"
git push origin main
```
```

5.4.9 Create GitHub Release

1. Run

    ```
    make release
    ```

2. Go to your GitHub repo ➤ Releases ➤ Draft new release.

3. Tag: v1.0.0 | Title: First Release.

4. Upload the generated binaries.

5. Add release notes.

6. Click **Publish** 🚀.

5.4.10 Recommended Project Structure

```
password-generator/
├── Makefile
├── LICENSE
├── README.md
├── go.mod
├── go.sum
├── main.go
├── password_test.go
└── password-generator (binary)
```

5.5 Summary

In this chapter, we

- Understood what CLI tools are

- Built a password generator CLI tool using Go

- Set up go mod for dependency management

- Used a Makefile for automation

- Documented and licensed the project

- Released the CLI tool on GitHub

These steps provide a foundational understanding of how to develop and share open source software in Go. In the next chapter, we will build and deploy a **simple web service in Go**. Stay tuned!

CHAPTER 6

Building and Deploying a Simple Web Service

6.1 Introduction

In the previous chapter, we built and released a command-line interface (CLI) tool. Now, we will enter the world of **web development** by creating and deploying a **simple RESTful web service** using Go.

In this chapter, you'll build a beginner-friendly yet practical project: a **URL Shortener Service**. It will help you

- Understand the basics of REST APIs

- Learn how Go handles HTTP servers

- Practice open source software development

- Deploy your web service to a cloud platform

© Rahul Sid Patil 2025
R. S. Patil, *Let Us Go!*, https://doi.org/10.1007/979-8-8688-1442-6_6

By the end of this chapter, you will

1. Understand what web services are and their typical use cases

2. Build a RESTful API in Go

3. Test your API using curl/Postman

4. Host it online using Render or Fly.io

5. Release the project as open source

6.2 Introduction to Web Services

6.2.1 🔍 What Is a Web Service?

A web service is a program that responds to **HTTP requests** to exchange data over the internet, usually in **JSON** or **XML** format.

6.2.2 🔧 Typical Use Cases

- Data sharing between systems

- Backend services for web/mobile apps

- Workflow automation (integrating third-party services)

6.2.3 🔖 Examples of Go-Based Web Services

- **Gitea**: Self-hosted Git platform

- **MinIO**: Object storage server

- **Traefik**: Cloud-native reverse proxy

- **Caddy**: Automatic HTTPS web server

6.3 Understanding Open Source Web Projects

The benefits and practices of open source software apply to web services too.

6.3.1 ☑ Why Open Source Your Web API?

- Encourages learning and collaboration
- Provides transparency
- Allows global contributions
- Adds credibility to your portfolio

6.3.2 ✎ Quick Best Practices

1. License your code (e.g., MIT).
2. Write clear README and API documentation.
3. Use GitHub for collaboration.

6.4 Step by Step: Build and Release a URL Shortener API in Go

6.4.1 ☺ Problem Statement

Build a **simple REST API** that shortens long URLs and redirects users from the short version to the original link.

6.4.2 Set Up Project Structure

1. **Create a GitHub Repository**

Replace yourusername with your actual GitHub username.

```
git clone https://github.com/yourusername/
url-shortener.git
cd url-shortener
go mod init github.com/yourusername/url-shortener
```

For example:

```
git clone https://github.com/rahulsidpatil/
url-shortener.git
cd url-shortener
go mod init github.com/rahulsidpatil/
url-shortener
```

2. **Project Structure**

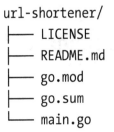

```
url-shortener/
├── LICENSE
├── README.md
├── go.mod
├── go.sum
└── main.go
```

6.4.3 Implement the Web Service

Create main.go:

```go
package main

import (
    "encoding/json"
    "fmt"
    "log"
    "math/rand"
    "net/http"
    "net/url"
    "sync"
    "time"
)

var (
    urlStore = make(map[string]string) // In-memory storage
    mu         sync.Mutex                 // Mutex for
                                          thread safety
)

func main() {
    rand.Seed(time.Now().UnixNano())
    http.HandleFunc("/shorten", shortenHandler)
    http.HandleFunc("/", redirectHandler)

    log.Println("Server started at :8080")
    if err := http.ListenAndServe(":8080", nil); err != nil {
        log.Fatalf("Server failed: %v", err)
    }
}

func shortenHandler(w http.ResponseWriter, r *http.Request) {
    if r.Method != http.MethodPost {
```

```go
        http.Error(w, "Method Not Allowed", http.
        StatusMethodNotAllowed)
        return
    }

    var req struct {
        URL string `json:"url"`
    }

    if err := json.NewDecoder(r.Body).Decode(&req);
    err != nil {
        http.Error(w, "Invalid JSON", http.StatusBadRequest)
        return
    }

    if _, err := url.ParseRequestURI(req.URL); err != nil {
        http.Error(w, "Invalid URL format", http.
        StatusBadRequest)
        return
    }

    short := generateShortURL()

    // Check for collisions (basic safeguard for demo)
    mu.Lock()
    for {
        if _, exists := urlStore[short]; !exists {
            break
        }
        short = generateShortURL()
    }
    urlStore[short] = req.URL
    mu.Unlock()
```

```go
    resp := map[string]string{"short_url": fmt.Sprintf
    ("http://localhost:8080/%s", short)}
    w.Header().Set("Content-Type", "application/json")
    json.NewEncoder(w).Encode(resp)
}

func redirectHandler(w http.ResponseWriter, r *http.Request) {
    short := r.URL.Path[1:]

    mu.Lock()
    longURL, exists := urlStore[short]
    mu.Unlock()

    if !exists {
        http.Error(w, "Short URL not found", http.
        StatusNotFound)
        return
    }

    http.Redirect(w, r, longURL, http.StatusFound)
}

func generateShortURL() string {
    const charset = "abcdefghijklmnopqrstuvwxyzABCDEFGHIJKLMNO
    PQRSTUVWXYZ0123456789"
    b := make([]byte, 6)
    for i := range b {
        b[i] = charset[rand.Intn(len(charset))]
    }
    return string(b)
}
```

☑ Sample Output (Local Testing Only)

```
$ curl -X POST http://localhost:8080/shorten \
```

```
-H "Content-Type: application/json" \
-d '{"url": "https://golang.org"}'
```

```
{"short_url":"http://localhost:8080/a1b2c3"}
```

Then test redirection:

```
$ curl -I http://localhost:8080/a1b2c3
```

⚠ **Note**   localhost URLs are only accessible on your local machine for testing purposes.

6.4.4 Add License and README

License: Use a permissive license like MIT.
README.md:

```
# URL Shortener Service

## Endpoints

### POST /shorten
Request:
```json
{ "url": "https://example.com" }
```

Response:

```json
{ "short_url": "http://localhost:8080/abc123" }
```
```

GET /abc123

Redirects to the original URL.

Run Locally

```bash
go run main.go
```

Contributing

Fork, commit changes, and open a pull request!

6.4.5 Deploy Your Service

You can deploy to Render, Fly.io, or Railway. Here's a quick start for Render:

render.yaml:

```
services:
  - type: web
    name: url-shortener
    env: go
    buildCommand: go build -o main .
    startCommand: ./main
```

Steps to Deploy

1. Push your project to GitHub.

2. Sign in to Render and connect your GitHub repo.

3. Choose Go as runtime and follow prompts to deploy.

ⓘ   You may also explore CI/CD workflows and container-based deployment for more control in production.

6.4.6 Test Using Postman (Optional but Recommended)

You can also test your API visually using Postman:

1. Create a POST request to `http://localhost:8080/shorten`.

2. In Body ➤ raw ➤ JSON:

    `{ "url": "https://example.com" }`

3. You'll get a JSON with `short_url`.

4. Test the redirection by visiting that short URL in a browser.

6.4.7 Add Security and Persistence Notes

⚠ **Security Warning**   This implementation accepts any URL, which can be exploited for phishing. Consider adding domain whitelisting and content validation.

🗄 **Persistence Tip**   The current solution uses in-memory map which loses data on restart. For production use, consider using Redis, PostgreSQL, or SQLite.

6.4.8 Create GitHub Release

1. Run

   ```
   go build -o url-shortener
   ```

2. Commit and push:

   ```
   git add .
   git commit -m "Initial release"
   git push origin main
   ```

3. Go to GitHub ➤ Releases ➤ Draft new release.

4. Tag it (e.g., v1.0.0), add release notes, and upload binary.

5. Click **Publish Release**.

6.5 Summary

In this chapter, you

- ☑ Learned how web services and REST APIs work

- ☑ Built a working URL shortener in Go

- ☑ Validated URLs and handled concurrency safely

- ☑ Added collision handling to short URL generation

- ☑ Wrote testable, maintainable Go code

- ☑ Added open source readiness (README, license)

- ☑ Tested via curl and Postman

- ☑ Deployed your API online

- ☑ Noted caveats about security and persistence

- ☑ Published the release to GitHub

🚀 **Next Steps**   Extend this project by adding analytics, TTL support, or persistent storage. Make it your own!

APPENDIX A

Golang Cheat Sheet

A concise, original reference guide covering essential Go concepts and syntax based entirely on the material presented in this book.

A.1 ⚒ Go Setup and Workspace Commands

```
go mod init <module-name>    # Initialize a Go module
go build                     # Compile your code
go run <file.go>             # Run a single file
go test                      # Run tests
go get <module-path>         # Add a dependency
```

A.2 ✦ Basic Program Structure

```
package main

import "fmt"

func main() {
    fmt.Println("Hello, Go!")
}
```
▶ Docs

© Rahul Sid Patil 2025
R. S. Patil, *Let Us Go!*, https://doi.org/10.1007/979-8-8688-1442-6

A.3 ⮔ Variables and Constants

```
var a int = 10
var b = "Hello"
c := 3.14 // Short declaration

const Pi = 3.14159
```

▶ Docs

A.4 🧠 Common Data Types

- **Basic**: int, float64, string, bool
- **Composite**: array, slice, map, struct, pointer, function, interface

```
var arr [3]int = [3]int{1, 2, 3}
s := []int{1, 2, 3}
m := map[string]int{"a": 1, "b": 2}
```

▶ Docs

A.5 🔁 Control Structures

A.5.1. If-Else

```
if x > 0 {
    fmt.Println("Positive")
} else {
    fmt.Println("Non-positive")
}
```

A.6 Switch

```
switch day {
case "Mon":
    fmt.Println("Monday")
default:
    fmt.Println("Other day")
}
```

A.7 For Loop

```
for i :- 0; i < 5; i++ {
    fmt.Println(i)
}
```
▶ Docs

A.8 ⟳ Functions

```
func add(a int, b int) int {
    return a + b
}
```

A.9 Multiple Return

```
func swap(x, y string) (string, string) {
    return y, x
}
```
▶ Docs

A.10 🎯 Structs and Methods

```go
type Person struct {
    Name string
    Age  int
}

func (p Person) Greet() {
    fmt.Println("Hi, I'm", p.Name)
}
```

▶ Docs

A.11 🌈 Arrays, Slices, Maps

A.11.1. Array

```go
arr := [3]int{1, 2, 3}
```

A.12 Slice

```go
s := []int{1, 2, 3}
s = append(s, 4)
```

A.13 Map

```go
m := map[string]int{"apple": 5, "banana": 7}
fmt.Println(m["apple"])
```

▶ Docs

A.14 🎁 Pointers

```
var p *int
x := 42
p = &x
fmt.Println("Address of x:", p)
fmt.Println("Value at p:", *p)
```

▶ Docs

A.15 📜 Goroutines and Channels

```
go sayHello()
ch := make(chan string)
go func() {
    ch <- "Hello!"
}()
msg := <-ch
fmt.Println(msg)
```

▶ Docs

A.16 🛡 Error Handling

```
val, err := strconv.Atoi("42")
if err != nil {
    log.Fatal(err)
}
```

▶ Docs

A.17 💼 Interfaces

```go
type Shape interface {
    Area() float64
}

type Circle struct {
    Radius float64
}

func (c Circle) Area() float64 {
    return math.Pi * c.Radius * c.Radius
}
```
▶ Docs

A.18 🧪 Testing in Go

```go
func Add(a, b int) int {
    return a + b
}
```

add_test.go

```go
import "testing"

func TestAdd(t *testing.T) {
    got := Add(2, 3)
    want := 5
    if got != want {
        t.Errorf("got %d, want %d", got, want)
    }
}
```
▶ Docs

A.19 🗀 Modules and Imports

```
go mod init github.com/username/project
```

```
go get github.com/example/pkg
go mod tidy
import "github.com/example/pkg"
```

▶ Docs

A.20 🔐 Defer, Panic, Recover

```go
func risky() {

    defer func() {
        if r := recover(); r != nil {
            fmt.Println("Recovered from:", r)
        }
    }()

    panic("Something went wrong!")
}

defer fmt.Println("This runs at the end")
```

▶ Docs

A.21 ✖ Go Tools Overview

- `go fmt`: Format code

- `go vet`: Detect suspicious constructs

- `go test`: Run unit tests

- `go mod tidy`: Sync dependencies

- `golint`: Enforce style (external)

A.22 ▥ Common Standard Library Packages

- `fmt`: Print formatting

- `math`: Basic math operations

- `strings`: String manipulation

- `strconv`: String<->int conversion

- `time`: Time/date handling

- `errors`: Error values

- `os, io`: File I/O (use instead of deprecated `io/ioutil`)

APPENDIX B

Golang Best Practices (Top 20)

Author: Rahul Sid Patil
Originally published on Stackademic
https://blog.stackademic.com/golang-quick-reference-top-20-best-coding-practices-c0cea6a43f20

B.1 Preface

This appendix is adapted from my original blog post published on Stackademic. As the sole author of the original article, I hold the rights to reuse, modify, and republish the content in this book. It has been refined and tailored specifically for readers of *Let Us Go Vol. 1* to serve as a handy reference to idiomatic and production-ready Go coding practices.

This appendix outlines the top 20 best coding practices in Go to help you write clear, idiomatic, and maintainable Go code. All examples align with the content taught throughout *Let Us Go Vol. 1*.

B.2 20. Use Proper Indentation

Consistent indentation improves readability:

```go
func main() {
    for i := 0; i < 5; i++ {
        fmt.Println("Hello, World!")
    }
}
```

Use gofmt to format your code automatically:

```
gofmt -w your_file.go
```

☑ **Takeaway**: Always run gofmt before committing code.

B.3 19. Import Packages Properly

Group imports logically: standard library, third-party, and internal packages.

```go
import (
    "fmt"
    "math/rand"
    "time"
)
```

☑ **Takeaway**: Remove unused imports with goimports or go mod tidy.

B.4 18. Use Descriptive Variable and Function Names

Use camelCase for variables and PascalCase for exported identifiers:

```
userName := "Alice"
itemCount := 5
isReady := true

func calculateSum(a, b int) int {
    return a + b
}
```

☑ **Takeaway**: Avoid abbreviations; choose names that describe intent.

B.5 17. Limit Line Length

Keep lines ≤ 120–150 characters to maintain readability.

☑ **Takeaway**: Break long statements across lines when necessary.

B.6 16. Use Constants for Magic Values

Avoid hardcoding values without context:

```
const (
    MaxRetries     = 3
    DefaultTimeout = 30
)
```

☑ **Takeaway**: Use iota for grouped constants when appropriate.

B.7 15. Handle Errors Explicitly

Always check and handle error returned by functions:

```
file, err := os.Open("example.txt")
if err != nil {
    log.Fatal(err)
}
```

☑ **Takeaway**: Avoid silent failures; be explicit and informative.

B.8 14. Avoid Global Variables

Encapsulate state within functions or structs:

```
func printMessage(msg string) {
    fmt.Println(msg)
}
```

☑ **Takeaway**: Globals make testing and debugging difficult.

B.9 13. Use Structs to Model Complex Data

Group related data fields into structs:

```
type Person struct {
    FirstName string
    LastName  string
    Age       int
}
```

☑ **Takeaway**: Structs are foundational for building clean APIs.

B.10 12. Comment Your Code

Follow the godoc style:

```
// greetUser returns a personalized greeting.
func greetUser(name string) string {
    return "Hello, " + name
}
```

☑ **Takeaway**: Write comments as if explaining to a future developer.

B.11 11. Use Goroutines for Concurrency

Use sync.WaitGroup to manage goroutine completion:

```
var wg sync.WaitGroup
wg.Add(1)
go func() {
    defer wg.Done()
    fmt.Println("Running concurrently")
}()
wg.Wait()
```

☑ **Takeaway**: Don't use time.Sleep for synchronization.

B.12 10. Handle Panics Gracefully

Use recover() inside deferred functions:

```
defer func() {
    if r := recover(); r != nil {
        fmt.Println("Recovered from panic:", r)
```

```
    }
}()
```

☑ **Takeaway**: Use panic only for truly unrecoverable conditions.

B.13 9. Avoid Overuse of `init()`

Prefer explicit initialization in main():

```
func setup() {
    fmt.Println("Initializing...")
}

func main() {
    setup()
    fmt.Println("App started")
}
```

☑ **Takeaway**: init() should be used only when truly required (e.g., rand. Seed()).

B.14 8. Use `defer` for Cleanup

Ensure resources are released:

```
file, err := os.Open("example.txt")
if err != nil {
    log.Fatal(err)
}
defer file.Close()
```

☑ **Takeaway**: Use defer immediately after acquiring a resource.

B.15 7. Prefer Composite Literals

Use struct literals instead of constructors when possible:

```go
person := Person{
    FirstName: "John",
    LastName:  "Doe",
    Age:       30,
}
```

☑ **Takeaway**: Improves readability and reduces boilerplate.

B.16 6. Minimize Function Parameters

Pass structs for related options:

```go
type ServerConfig struct {
    Port    int
    Timeout int
}
```

☑ **Takeaway**: Fewer parameters = simpler testing and maintenance.

B.17 5. Prefer Explicit Return Values

Avoid named returns unless absolutely necessary:

```go
func sum(a, b int) int {
    return a + b
}
```

☑ **Takeaway**: Explicit > implicit when clarity matters.

B.18 4. Keep Functions Small and Focused

Break logic into smaller functions:

```go
func calculateSum(a, b int) int {
    return a + b
}
```

☑ **Takeaway**: A function should do one thing and do it well.

B.19 3. Avoid Variable Shadowing

Use unique variable names to prevent confusion:

```go
x := 10
{
    y := 5 // instead of reusing `x`
    fmt.Println(y)
}
```

☑ **Takeaway**: Shadowing leads to hard-to-trace bugs.

B.20 2. Use Interfaces for Abstraction

Interfaces decouple implementation from usage:

```go
type Shape interface {
    Area() float64
}
```

☑ **Takeaway**: Interfaces simplify testing and extension.

B.21 1. Separate Executables and Libraries

Organize projects with clear separation between main and library code:

```
myproject/
├── main.go
└── utils/
    └── helpers.go
```

☑ **Takeaway**: Keep business logic in packages, not in main.go.

By following these practices, you can ensure that your Go programs are clean, idiomatic, and production-ready.

APPENDIX C

Golang Is Written in Go—How?

Author: Rahul Sid Patil
Originally published on Stackademic
https://blog.stackademic.com/golang-is-written-using-golang-how-830f9cfa4eb2

C.1 Preface

This appendix is adapted from my original blog post published on Stackademic. As the sole author of the original article, I hold the rights to reuse, modify, and republish the content in this book. It has been refined and tailored specifically for readers of *Let Us Go Vol. 1* to serve as a handy reference to idiomatic and production-ready Go coding practices.

C.2 Introduction

One of the most fascinating facts about Go is that its compiler is primarily written in Go itself. But how is that even possible? How can a language be compiled by a compiler that's written in the same language?

© Rahul Sid Patil 2025
R. S. Patil, *Let Us Go!*, https://doi.org/10.1007/979-8-8688-1442-6

In this appendix, we'll explore the clever **bootstrapping process** that made this possible, understand why the Go team pursued this path, and appreciate the philosophy and design principles it reflects.

C.3 The Bootstrapping Process

Bootstrapping in programming languages refers to the process of writing a compiler in the language it is meant to compile. It sounds paradoxical—like trying to pull yourself up by your own bootstraps—but in the world of systems programming, it's a well-established and elegant method.

Go's compiler didn't start out written in Go. The journey was iterative, strategic, and deliberate.

C.4 Timeline of Bootstrapping

```
[C Compiler (Original 'gc')]
         ↓
[Minimal Go Runtime + GC]
         ↓
[Go Compiler in Go]
         ↓
[Full Self-Hosting Compiler]
```

C.5 Starting with C

The initial Go compiler—known as gc—was implemented in **C**. This bootstrap compiler was capable of compiling a minimal subset of the Go language. It allowed the Go team to lay the groundwork for the language's runtime and garbage collector.

C.6 Implementing Minimal Runtime and Garbage Collection

The subset of Go that the C-based compiler could handle was just enough to build

- A **basic runtime** (memory management, scheduling, etc.)

- A **simple garbage collector**

These foundational pieces enabled the team to begin building more of the language using Go itself.

C.7 Writing Go in Go

Once the initial runtime was in place, the Go team started implementing the Go compiler **in Go itself**. This new Go-based compiler was capable of compiling a wider subset of the language, gradually replacing its C-based predecessor.

C.8 Iterative Self-Hosting

With each iteration, more of the language was rewritten in Go:

- Expanded compiler capabilities

- More packages in the standard library

- Enhanced runtime support

Eventually, this process led to a compiler that could fully compile itself—the Go compiler written in Go.

☑ The fully self-hosted compiler replaced the old gc compiler as of **Go 1.5 (2015)**.

C.9 Full Self-Sufficiency Achieved

At this point, Go achieved **self-hosting**:

- The Go compiler was now **written in Go**.

- The Go compiler **compiled itself**.

- Go releases no longer required a C compiler.

This marked a significant milestone in the language's maturity and portability.

C.10 Why Did Go Take This Approach?

C.10.1 ⬧ Simplicity and Self-Containment

Go was designed to be

- Minimal

- Easy to maintain

- Pragmatic in real-world development

A self-hosted compiler reinforces these goals.

C.11 ✹ Cross-Platform Portability

Using C as the initial compiler made Go bootstrappable across systems. But once the Go-based compiler was ready, it enabled the toolchain to run anywhere Go could run—no external dependencies required.

C.12 🔁 Accelerated Language Evolution

A compiler written in Go made it easier to

- Add language features
- Improve error messages
- Optimize the build process

And do it all **within the language ecosystem itself**.

C.13 Conclusion

The fact that **Go is written in Go** is a testament to its thoughtful design, practical implementation, and the vision of its creators.

The bootstrapping process demonstrates how a modern programming language can evolve from humble beginnings to full self-sufficiency—a process that showcases both engineering rigor and elegance.

So as you write and compile your Go programs, remember

💡 You're using a language that pulled itself up by its own bootstraps—and did so beautifully.

Index

© Rahul Sid Patil 2025
R. S. Patil, *Let Us Go!*, https://doi.org/10.1007/979-8-8688-1442-6

H

I, J, K